/FOURTH EDITION/

STUDY GUIDE

EFFECTIVE
POLICE
SUPERVISION

LARRY S. MILLER / MICHAEL C. BRASWELL
WITH JACKIE CHAPMAN

EAST TENNESSEE STATE UNIVERSITY

anderson publishing co.
2035 Reading Road
Cincinnati, OH 45202
800-582-7295

Effective Police Supervision, Fourth Edition — Study Guide

Copyright © 1990, 1996, 1999, 2003
Anderson Publishing Co.
2035 Reading Rd.
Cincinnati, OH 45202

Phone 800.582.7295 or 513.421.4142
Web Site www.andersonpublishing.com

ISBN: 1-583690953-X

Cover design by Tin Box Studio, Inc.

EDITOR Ellen S. Boyne
ACQUISITIONS EDITOR Michael C. Braswell

A Note to the Student

This Study Guide was created to complement *Effective Police Supervision*, **Fourth Edition by Harry W. More, W. Fred Wegener, and Larry S. Miller**. It is not designed to serve as a substitute for the textbook. You will need to read the book to fully understand the concepts of effective police supervision, and you will need the textbook to complete portions of this Guide.

The best strategy before reading each chapter of the textbook is to look at this Study Guide first. Read the Learning Objectives and Key Concepts. These will help you focus on key material as you read the text. After reading the chapter in the text it may be helpful to outline the chapter, and it will be useful to write out definitions and/or examples for each of the Key Concepts listed. You may wish to include other terms and concepts from the text that are not listed in the Guide.

Your professor may assign particular Discussion Topics and Questions or Case Studies from the text. Thinking about and crafting responses to the issues raised in these questions and scenarios, whether or not they are formally assigned, will help you to grasp key concepts and synthesize the material in a meaningful and applicable way that goes beyond learning by rote. Finally, the questions and answer key provided in this Guide will provide one way for you to measure how well you are grasping the material.

We hope this Guide proves helpful in your studies of police supervision. If you have comments on how the Guide can be improved for future editions or if you find mistakes, please send them to: Anderson Publishing Co., Criminal Justice Division, 2035 Reading Rd., Cincinnati, OH 45202.

Contents

Chapter 1
Supervision—
The Management Task

Learning Objectives

1. Identify the skills needed by a first-line supervisor.

2. Define *knowledge-based skills*.

3. Identify *human skills*.

4. Compare *conceptual* and *affective skills*.

5. Describe a positive attitude toward management's expectations of the supervisor.

6. Define *loyalty*.

7. Characterize the subordinate's expectations of the supervisor.

8. Identify the key elements of participation.

9. Describe the process of conflict resolution.

10. List the functions performed by supervisors when relating to subordinates.

Key Concepts

affective skills
analytical approach
conceptual skills
conflict resolution
dynamic organization
human skills
integrity
knowledge-based skills
loyalty
management expectations of the supervisor

officer behavior
participation
peer expectations of the supervisor
performance
positive attitude
responding to management
self-appraisal
subordinate expectations of the supervisor
supervisory skill areas
transition

Chapter Summary

I. Transformation

The first-line supervisor is at the organizational focal point between line officers and other police managers. It is important to learn the positive aspects of reaching the position of first-line supervisor and also to be able to understand why the first-line supervisor's position is not for everyone by examining the negative aspects of the position. Good supervisors do not just happen; they must be cultivated. The first-line supervisor has become an important part of management who is responsible for improving the quality of work life.

Police work has become more and more complex, and it seems reasonable that problems facing today's officers will only increase with the complexity of the job. The supervisor must respond with imagination and innovation. One of the most difficult of the new duties facing the supervisor is being an effective disciplinarian. The supervisor must learn to meet the needs of both officers and the organization, developing a wide range of skills.

II. Supervisory Skills Areas

Once an officer assumes the position of first-line supervisor, his or her role changes drastically and tasks become managerial. It is a supervisor's responsibility to emphasize the development of subordinates' skills rather than doing everything him or herself. In order to maximize effectiveness, a supervisor must attain objectives through the efforts of others by becoming operationally effective in one or more of the following skill areas:

A. *Knowledge-based skills.* The supervisor has the ability to handle the administrative responsibilities and provides the technical support that each officer needs. The supervisor has the knowledge of the policies and procedures and implements them effectively. The supervisor is responsible for the training and development of the officers.

B. *Human skills.* An effective supervisor has the ability to be able to listen effectively and discuss problems with subordinates and deal with each officer as an individual. The effective supervisor also sets the standard of professionalism by example and encourages a positive attitude through individual encouragement and motivation of the employees. This supervisor has the ability to resolve conflicts effectively.

C. *Conceptual skills.* The supervisor has the ability to analyze situations and make good decisions. Also, the supervisor is capable of integrating personal activities into the total organizational plan so that agency goals are attained.

D. *Affective skills.* The supervisor acts as a role model by demonstrating both integrity and loyalty. Moreover, the supervisor demonstrates the ability to integrate organizational values and community values. An environment that is based on equality and fairness is developed, which demonstrates that the supervisor values the employees and their contribution to the organization.

The supervisor should do a **self-appraisal** to select managerial techniques that fit his or her style. It is also important to understand line officers and their potential, acknowledging individual differences and cultivating the talents of officers. This style of supervision allows the supervisor to arrive at decisions suitable for the employee and the organization. However, supervisors must be flexible in their approaches and recognize that a particular approach does not work every time.

Managerial networking involves flexibility in combining different supervisory approaches. Each officer should be integrated into the organization, and the focus on decision making improves work life and productivity. The purpose of networking is to foster self-help, exchange information, and share resources.

III. Management Expectations of the Supervisor

To meet managerial expectations of the supervisor, the supervisor must develop the ability to identify duties that relate to the management of people and emphasize them. The importance of a supervisor maintaining a **positive attitude** as a means of dealing with obstacles in a constructive manner cannot be stressed enough. A first-line supervisor must also maintain **loyalty** to upper management. When one accepts a supervisory position, one accepts the obligation to be part of the team. Management should expect the **performance** of its supervisors to be excellent. Tasks and responsiblities should be handled in a timely and professional manner. However, when a timetable cannot realistically be met, this must be conveyed and dealt with. **Responding to management** is vital. Management expects the first-line supervisor to maintain a high level of communication with them, especially to keep them aware of subordinates' concerns, desires, and suggestions. They also expect the supervisor to have the ability to efficiently prepare administrative paperwork, i.e., budget requests, assigned investigations, and written employee evaluations.

As with subordinates, first-line supervisors must look on management as made up of unique individuals. They need to identify their managers' strengths and weaknesses, work habits, and needs—and then respond accordingly. Supervisors need to be viewed by management as helpful colleagues and trustworthy professionals who are part of the management team.

IV. Subordinate Expectations of the Supervisor

First-line supervisors have to deal with demands from both within and outside the agency. The primary reason for the supervisory position is the need for work to be accomplished effectively. For the organization to continue to exist, goals must be achieved.

Subordinates' needs must be recognized and met by the organization. When the needs are met by the job, then the job motivates the employee. This must be continuously assessed by the supervisor. The authors state that 85 percent of employees will respond to the positive efforts of the supervisor, but that the greater amount of a supervisor's time is usually spent on the remaining 15 percent who, for whatever reason, are "poor employees."

Authoritarian management should be discarded. The changed attitude of police officers has shown that they will give their best for a certain number of hours if they have a positive work environment. Today's officers look for a challenging job, an opportunity to make a contribution, self-expression, and free time for outside activities.

A. *Participative management.* The process of opening the decision-making process up to employees to participate. The employee must be empowered in order to accomplish assigned tasks; thus, power must be shared. This participative management may reduce the number of traditional managers needed, but will increase the need for leaders. The end result is an environment in which officers want to work.

B. *Conflict resolution.* The ability of the supervisor to assist subordinates with problems that are both internal and external to the department while being able to distinguish between real employee complaints and petty bickering or mere griping. Conflict identification and resolution are considered by many supervisors to be the most important function of the first-line supervisor.

V. Peer Expectations of the Supervisor

Supervision is a joint effort between supervisors in order to successfully accomplish the tasks and goals of the organization. Reciprocal, positive relationships between peers require communication and consideration. The first-line supervisor must learn the importance and effectiveness of "end-of-shift" communication between supervisors. They must also learn the value of conferences or staff meetings and utilize them as a means to provide adequate time for discussion in matters that require a complete understanding of the organization's position on procedures and policies. Successful worker relationships focus on the work rather than personalities. The ability to get along with people is the hallmark of the professional. Supervisors should deal with any inevitable criticisms in a constructive manner.

Case Study Exercises/Essays

1. Assume you are Sergeant Clark:
   a. What would you do to resolve the problem?
   b. What would you do to ensure you perform well as a supervisor?

2. Assume you are Sergeant Martin:
   a.   Would you go to your supervisor and ask for help?
   b.   Would you ask the people you are supervising for suggestions on how to improve your performance?

Multiple-Choice Questions (Circle the best answer)

1. According to More, Wegener, and Miller, first-line supervisors are:
   a.   a non-integral part of management.
   b.   indirectly responsible for improving the quality of working life.
   c.   an integral part of management.
   d.   a necessary evil.

2. _____ is what most first-line supervisors deal with in the workplace. The greater the supervisor's knowledge in this area, the greater the prospect that both individual and organizational goals will be attained.
   a.   Paperwork
   b.   Discipline
   c.   Task selection
   d.   Human behavior

3. If supervisors are successful in the performance of their duties:
   a.   they will quickly be promoted.
   b.   the organization will become more effective.
   c.   they will play a minor role in responding to change that affects the organization.
   d.   they will receive additional training within one year after being promoted.

4. Transition from a line position to a first-line supervisor means that, administratively, supervisors:
   a.   should distance themselves from officers.
   b.   should not be involved in the decision-making process.
   c.   must not become a part of management.
   d.   usually head a given operation and become a part of management.

5. The transition to the position of first-line supervisor:
   a.   presents little challenge.
   b.   demands the ability to accept and adapt to change.
   c.   should be accomplished with very little effort.
   d.   may never be attained if the ecology of the organization is known.

6. The human skills approach deals with:
   a.   emotions, agency goals, values.
   b.   attitudes, interpretation, analysis.
   c.   analysis, interpretation, resolution.
   d.   emotions, values, attitudes.

7. The analytical approach deals with:
   a.   emotions, agency goals, values.
   b.   attitudes, interpretation, analysis.
   c.   analysis, interpretation, resolution.
   d.   emotions, values, attitudes.

8. Supervisors demonstrating knowledge-based skills will:
    a. provide officers with appropriate administrative and technical support.
    b. possibly consider each officer's workload, but not as a priority.
    c. show an interest in seeing that their officers carry out an assignment if time permits.
    d. implement departmental policies and procedures at all costs.

9. In order for supervisors to accomplish work through people, they must:
    a. know the capabilities and limitations of each employee.
    b. apply different standards for each employee.
    c. set standards higher than capabilities to build in challenge for employees.
    d. all of the above

10. Supervisors demonstrating human skills should:
    a. not discuss problems with subordinates.
    b. perform as professionals and set the standards for employees.
    c. order officers to get counseling when problems arise.
    d. encourage peer pressure as a means of motivation.

11. The first-line supervisor is in the best position to _____ and _____ conflicts between specialized police units by using conceptualization techniques.
    a. identify and assess
    b. assess and discipline
    c. discipline and resolve
    d. identify and resolve

12. When a new policy or general order is promulgated, the best way to react is to:
    a. distribute the written policy to subordinates and refrain from any discussion.
    b. distribute the written policy and point out the weaknesses in the policy so that the subordinates know the problems with implementation.
    c. distribute the policy and any positive or negative research that you have received on the change so that the subordinates recognize that you are knowledgeable about the new policy.
    d. be honest with your subordinates and tell them when the policy is a poor one so they will respect you.
    e. be positive; distribute the policy and respond based on a critical evaluation of ways that will ensure the policy is workable.

13. First-line supervisors are at the fulcrum between management and line operations and therefore must:
    a. identify problem employees to upper management immediately.
    b. accomplish the tasks of interpreting rules, regulations, and policies.
    c. insulate themselves from undue influence from above and below.
    d. find out about problems with subordinates first so that discipline can be given and the supervisor will look favorable to upper management.

14. In the case study, Sergeant Dale demonstrated predominantly _____ supervisory skills.
    a. knowledge-based
    b. human
    c. conceptual
    d. affective

15. A failure by a subordinate to perform at acceptable levels must be:
    a. confronted and resolved in favor of the organization.
    b. reviewed by the supervisor and then standards must be reevaluated to fit the individual needs of the employee.
    c. resolved with discipline to set an example for the rest.
    d. ignored and the employee watched for improvement over time.

16. In order for officers to feel a part of the organization:
    a. they should be allowed to achieve individual needs even if agency needs are put on hold.
    b. satisfying organizational goals must be their focus.
    c. they should be included in the decision-making process across the board.
    d. job satisfaction should be accomplished by allowing officers to achieve individual needs while organizational needds are satisfied.

17. Progressive police agencies open the decision-making process to:
    a. all employees.
    b. employees who are loyal to the administrators.
    c. employees who have firsthand knowledge and are allowed to study problems confronting the agency.
    d. first-line supervisors and above in rank structure.

18. The real by-product of participative management is that it:
    a. shifts the burden off top administrators.
    b. creates a work environment in which officers want to work.
    c. requires more supervisors to get the job done.
    d. requires an overhaul of human nature.

19. Successful accomplishment of tasks and goal attainment requires:
    a. no consideration given as to how the supervisor's actions affect the duties of others.
    b. coordination and cooperation between supervisors.
    c. a strict code of order-giving and follow-up.
    d. that the supervisor report only to the chief to avoid miscommunication.

20. Successful dealings with peers require:
    a. management by discipline.
    b. information-hoarding.
    c. independent problem solving.
    d. joint resolution of problems.

21. The authors stress that a positive method for discussion before the implementation of a new policy is the:
    a. end-of-shift briefing.
    b. beginning-of-shift briefing.
    c. conference setting.
    d. memorandum of understanding.

True or False Questions

_F_   1. It is necessary for a supervisor to consider both the social needs of the officers and the tasks to be performed.

T   2. The transition to the position of first-line supervisor is fraught with difficulty for most individuals.

T   3. Good supervision is the result of the serious application of one's knowledge about human behavior to the work situation.

T   4. A first-line supervisor must become personally acquainted with each employee and treat them as individuals.

T   5. According to More, Wegener, and Miller, middle and top management want to feel that rules are supported by first-line supervisors.

F   6. Supervisors should be able to stereotype the manager in order to better understand that manager's management methods.

F   7. An effective first-line supervisor will identify his or her own style of management and stick with it no matter what the individual situation presents, in order to show consistency.

T   8. First-line supervisors should project an air of caring by being constantly available for help and guidance and accepting and resolving problems as they occur, while exhibiting a genuine desire to trust each employee.

F   9. First-line supervisors must learn that employee complaints are just gripe sessions for the employee and require no supervisory action

T   10. According to More, Wegener, and Miller, the supervisor's position is one of conflict identification and resolution.

T   11. Focusing on the work to be done rather than the personalities of those involved results in positive relationships with peers.

T   12. A supervisor's success depends on the qualities and qualifications brought to the managerial process and the method used in resolving conflict.

T   13. The ability to get along with people is the hallmark of the professional and a sign of maturity.

T   14. Individuals who think positively are results-oriented and deal with obstacles in a constructive manner.

F   15. According to More, Wegener, and Miller, middle and top management expectations of the first-line supervisor include a positive attitude, accomplishment of tasks, and responding to requests from upper management, but there is little concern about loyalty to the department.

Chapter 2
Community Policing—
Serving the Neighborhoods

Learning Objectives

1. Define *community policing*.

2. Describe the importance of *empowerment*.

3. List the responsibilities of a first-line supervisor in community policing.

4. Describe how a supervisor should build partnerships within the department.

5. Define *collaboration*.

6. List eight different potential resources for problem solving.

7. Identify some of the elements of quality supervision.

8. Define *process facilitation*.

9. Describe the typical day of community policing supervisor.

10. List and define the four components of problem solving.

11. List several reasons why one should manage failure.

Key Concepts

actors	partnerships
analysis	problem solving
assessment	process facilitation
collaboration	quality supervision
community enhancement	response
community policing success	risk taking
empowerment	scanning
environmental surveys	sequence of events
incidents	social context
institutional	supervisory techniques
managing failure	third parties
offenders	victims

Chapter Summary

I. Community Policing—What Is It?

Community policing is a philosophy of policing in which the officers work closely with the community residents. This is accomplished by the officers having informal contacts with residents and institutions serving the area. Community policing lets law enforcement officials address not only the crime, but its causes. Along with identifying problems, the department can focus community resources to solve the problems. To be successful, top management must express the values and mission of community policing to all levels within the organization.

II. Empowerment

The five identified characteristics of officers and supervisors operating in a community policing organization are:

1.   Risk taking
2.   Originality
3.   Creativity
4.   Individuality
5.   Problem solving

A. *Empowerment.* This is the conscious decision of the chief executive officer to allow others to assume decision making through delegated power and authority.

The supervisor's role requires that he or she coach, support, and help officers in planning, analyzing, and solving community problems.

B. *Quality supervision.* Involves shared decision making, teamwork, creativity, and innovation.

III. Process Facilitation

The first-line supervisor is responsible for conveying the importance of community policing to the police officers. The officers need to be shown that involvement in the community and problem solving are **real** work.

A. *Process facilitator.* A supervisor who communicates openly, becomes a team member, and encourages officers to participate actively in problem solving.

When the first-line supervisor accomplishes becoming a process facilitator, he or she can effectively serve as a conduit to relay information up the chain of command. It is imperative to the success of the community policing program to build **partnerships** within the agency. Through these partnerships come resources to solve the problems as they become identified. The first-line supervisor must "sell" the problems to all units and foster a relationship that assures commitment to the cause.

IV. Collaboration

For community policing to work, a wide range of resources must be used to solve problems. Identification of resources and development of collaborative efforts are essential. Line officers should have a means for requesting services (see Figure 2.4). Supervisors should monitor and evaluate the collaboration process. Liaison and follow-up are essential to the success of collaboration.

V. Problem Solving

The modern approach to problem solving is a positive orientation that is proactive in nature. Thus, problems are viewed from the perspective of the entire community. Citizens, police departments, and other agencies unite to work proactively in identifying community problems and in correcting them. Within the police department, detectives and line officers use the problem solving approach to identify, analyze, and respond to factors that often lead to citizen complaints or requests for help.

The four components of problem solving are:

1.   **Scanning** — identifies the problems and prioritizes them. The scanning phase also involves the assignment of personnel.
2.   **Analysis** — learning what the problem's causes and effects are. Analysis involves the collection of all available information (including actors and incidents).
3.   **Response** — initiating actions to either correct or alleviate the problem. May involve engaging the resources of other community agencies or resources.
4.   **Assessment** — process of determining the effectiveness of the response. May involve the administration of a community survey to gather information on attitudes and opinions toward the police response.

VI. Supervising Community Policing Officers

The authoritative style of supervision is not conducive to managing a community policing officer—officers must be given greater control over their work environment. A few rewards for community policing officers are:

1.   They have greater control over the work performed.
2.   They have increased responsibility for the work performed and increased autonomy.
3.   They have direct involvement in the decision-making process, due to the increased participation in problem solving.

Therefore, it appears that community policing officers can obtain greater job satisfaction. The first-line supervisor becomes more of a resource person and manager for the officers. First-line supervisors must spend time with the officers in the neighborhood if they are to be able to help the officers with the community problems they face.

VII. Managing Failure

Managing in a community police environment must be done in an informal manner. This is because this problem-solving approach is a new technique for officers. The supervisors must accept that they will make mistakes and that failures will occur. It is the supervisor's responsibility to manage and control those failures so that positive results can ultimately occur. Documenting the failures is important also, so that this information can be shared with other interested people. This will allow the agency to identify areas that need training. A teamwork philosophy must prevail if community policing is to be successful.

A. *Managing failure.* This is a process of depersonalizing failure and judging the actual event and not the involved individual.

It is important for the supervisor to realize that failure should lead to growth and not negative discipline for the officer.

Case Study Exercises/Essays

1. Assume you are Sergeant Horton:

   a. What would you do when you got together with your team?
   b. What information would you want from the department?
   c. What would you do to create a good working arrangement with the neighborhood association?

2. Assume you are Sergeant Gomez:

   a. How could you create a positive work environment?
   b. How would you get the support personnel involved in the team effort?

Multiple-Choice Questions (Circle the best answer)

1. All but which of the following are true in relation to community policing?
   a. It grabs headlines throughout the nation.
   b. There is a consensus in defining it.
   c. Police conferences discuss it in depth.
   d. Special training can prepare officers to carry out problem-solving programs.

2. Community policing is a process in which the police become:
   a. loners.
   b. beat cops.
   c. protectors, organizers, and advocates.
   d. focused on new-age techniques to achieve peace.

3. All but which of the following are true about the working definition of community policing?
   a. Officers work jointly with community residents.
   b. Consideration is given to the needs of the community.
   c. The police work to solve a community's problems for them.
   d. The causes of crime are agreed upon.

4. An essential ingredient of community policing is:
   a. empowerment of officers and first-line supervisors.
   b. involvement of upper management.
   c. increased funding.
   d. flexibility of shift assignments.

5. With the introduction of community policing, the _____ is/are at the focal point of change.
   a. chief executive officer
   b. residents and business owners
   c. community policing officers
   d. first-line supervisors

6. Quality supervisors must personify the attributes of a/an_____ if community policing is to succeed.
   a. communicator and an authoritarian
   b. authoritarian and a role model
   c. facilitator and a coach
   d. coach and an authoritarian

7. During the facilitation process, the supervisor must do all of the following except:
    a. take on the task of independent problem solving.
    b. convince police officers that community engagement and problem solving are real police work.
    c. genuinely support organizational changes.
    d. articulate and reinforce the philosophy of community policing.

8. Responsibilities of a first-line supervisor for supervising community policing officers include:
    a. personalizing failures and judging the individual officer to decide if the officer is fit for the program.
    b. encouraging officers not to take risks, but to discuss problems with the supervisor before acting.
    c. ensuring the retention of beat integrity when problem solving.
    d. discouraging inventiveness when problem solving.

9. Supervisors can reinforce the collaboration process of problem solving by:
    a. requiring detailed paperwork.
    b. checking the efforts of officers.
    c. requiring notification of every effort.
    d. using a "hands-off" approach that encourages independence.

10. Failure should lead to:
    a. a review board.
    b. growth.
    c. punishment.
    d. reparation.

11. All but which of the following describe the first-line supervisor's functions under empowerment?
    a. mentor
    b. manipulator
    c. motivator
    d. facilitator

12. The first phase of the problem-solving approach is:
    a. searching.
    b. seeking.
    c. scanning.
    d. scope.

True or False Questions

_F_ 1. Philosophically, community policing is an insignificant change in the provision of police services.

_T_ 2. Community policing gives officers an opportunity to move closer to the community.

_T_ 3. Community policing is a process in which the officers become organizers, advocates, and protectors.

_T_ 4. Community policing, to be successful, demands radical changes over time if there is to be significant alteration in the way the organization attains goals.

_F_ 5. In community policing, line officers and supervisors are the recipients of a minor shift of power and authority.

_F_   6.   Empowerment occurs when the supervisor encourages officers to "stay out of trouble" or "not bother" their sergeant.

_F_   7.   When empowerment occurs, community policing is doomed.

_T_   8.   Supervisors must convey to all officers the importance of community policing and that it is real police work.

_T_   9.   Under community policing, isolation between officers and detectives must always be reduced.

_F_   10. The chief executive officer is the key to community policing and all other units should support the problem-solving efforts.

_T_   11. Monitoring and responding to citizen complaints affects the credibility of the line officers and the police department.

_T_   12. Community policing involves giving officers greater control over their working conditions.

_F_   13. The first-line supervisor must manage in a formal manner in order to avoid mistakes.

_F_   14. When managing failure, a first-line supervisor must personalize the failure of the community policing officer and evaluate the individual officer to decide if he or she is fit to belong to the unit.

_T_   15. The importance of collaboration in community policing is that it can provide a variety of resources to resolve identifiable problems.

_F_   16. The analysis component of the problem-solving approach involves identification of a community problem.

_T_   17. The problem-solving approach may assess the effectiveness of community policing through public surveys.

Chapter 3
Interpersonal Communication—
Striving for Effectiveness

Learning Objectives

1. List the reasons a first-line supervisor should become a skillful communicator.

2. Identify, in order of importance, the tasks performed by a supervisor.

3. Define *interpersonal communication*.

4. Describe the elements of the realistic communication process.

5. Compare one-way and two-way communication.

6. Identify the major barriers to the communication process.

7. Describe how to overcome communication barriers.

8. Identify the ways a supervisor can provide positive feedback.

9. Describe the techniques a supervisor can use to improve listening skills.

10. Identify the key characteristics of body language.

11. Describe the importance of paralanguage and facial expressions when communicating.

12. Discuss how diversity training may benefit officers.

13. List things an officer can do when communicating with hearing-impaired individuals.

Key Concepts

art of listening
communicating with non-English-speaking individuals
communication patterns
communication process
decoding
encoding
feedback
hearing impairment
importance of communications
intercultural communications
interpreters
lip-reading

nonverbal communication
one-way communication
overcoming communication barriers
paralanguage
physical barriers
proxemics
psychological barriers
realistic communication process
semantics
simplistic communication process
two-way communication

Chapter Summary

I. The Importance of Communication Skills

The ability to communicate effectively is a prerequisite to being a successful supervisor. As the tasks performed by the first-line supervisor become more complex, it is imperative that a supervisor develop excellent communication skills. Interpersonal communication exists at all levels of management. However, the first-line supervisor interacts continually with officers at the operational level. The first-line supervisor is the primary communication point between upper management and the line officer.

Of 53 representative tasks a first-line supervisor completes, 51 percent of those tasks involve communication. The effectiveness of communication depends on the communicator's awareness of communication needs and the ability to express an idea clearly and influence another person.

II. The Communication Process

Communication is the exchange of information between people. Effective communication involves transmission of a message, decoding the message, and the recipient correctly interpreting and understanding the message. This communication process is exceedingly complex when you factor in attitudes, skills, knowledge, opinions and other preexisting factors. *Gatekeeping* refers to the sender determining the relevance and importance of information. Because of operational autonomy, the first-line supervisor is in a position to control the amount and nature of information entering the system.

The elements of a realistic communication process include: sender, encoding, channel, decoding, receiver, noise, and feedback (see Figure 3.3). Content and context are also important considerations in effective communication.

There can be one-way communication, such as an order to act, or two-way communication, where there is an exchange.

A. *One-way communication.* The communicator sends out a message. Traditionally, this has dominated police supervisory techniques with subordinates.

One-way communication is preferred when speed and compliance are imperative and orderliness is significant. It protects the sender's authority and power because errors are never acknowledged. This is frequently used in SWAT team environments.

B. *Two-way communication.* Two-way communication occurs when the recipient provides feedback to the sender. Two-way communication improves accuracy of the message and provides a greater understanding. However, with two-way communication the sender must share the power and authority.

III. Barriers to Communication

There are always barriers to communication, which can be either *physical* or *psychological*. Barriers generally involve concern about one's knowledge of the subject, the possibility of being looked upon with displeasure, jeopardizing one's status, environmental influences, personal expectations, and *semantics*. Because subordinates are careful not to affect their personal position with the supervisor, barriers that impede open two-way communication are formed.

IV. Overcoming Communication Barriers

Supervisors must recognize that barriers do exist. They need to attempt to develop a supportive relationship with subordinates if they are going to be able to evaluate the situations that arise. Real two-way communication exists when subordinates accept a supervisor as someone who helps and supports rather than one who forces, demands, or orders.

V. Feedback

A. *Feedback.* Information received by the sender from the recipient so that the sender may modify and correct the initial message. Feedback is most beneficial when used as a way to help the recipient understand communication.

Feedback works best in an environment based on developed relationships and trust. For feedback to be most effective, it should be selective, specific, descriptive, issue-oriented, and based on fact rather than personality. Because even constructive criticism is difficult to face, supervisors should provide feedback at an appropriate time and place. The ultimate goal is improved communication and performance. Furthermore, feedback should also contribute to an individuals knowledge about their performance.

VI. The Art of Listening

The effective supervisor has the responsibility to develop the skill of listening. Listening is an active process. A good listener makes every attempt to get the message. When a supervisor listens to a subordinate, that employee must be made to feel that no one will be allowed to interrupt their conversation. Listeners must always keep an open mind and recognize their own biases. They must not let their personal feelings prevent communication. If the supervisor as listener addresses situations intellectually, it allows officers' ideas to be heard. Listeners must look for implications to get clues about what is really being said. This requires the listener to stop talking and hear what is being said.

VII. Nonverbal Communication

Nonverbal communication includes the stance, gestures, facial expressions, and other nonverbal cues used when delivering a message. It is primarily used to convey emotions, desires, and preferences. The face is the main communicator of emotions.

Eye contact can be used very effectively to control communication. It reinforces talking with an employee because it demonstrates that the employee has the supervisor's undivided attention. A supervisor who can effectively use nonverbal communication can use cues to support and reinforce communication, and this will reduce the possibility of the recipient misinterpreting the sender's message.

Nonverbal communication can also be conveyed through paralanguage, which is voice volume, tone, pitch, and/or inflection.

VIII. Communicating with Non-English-Speaking Individuals

When attempting to communicate with a non-English-speaking individual, an officer should try to hire an individual who can serve as a translator. The translator may be a family member, neighbor, fellow officer, or other agency member.

IX. Intercultural Communication

Becoming educated in intercultural communications improves communication between police officers and individuals of different cultural backgrounds. Such training allows officers to be sensitive to the etiquette, traditions, and communication styles of other cultures.

X. Communicating with Hearing-Impaired Individuals

It is estimated that 21 million people in the United States have a hearing impairment. Individuals with a hearing impairment can be identified through careful observation. Once the impairment is identified, the officer communicating should face the person directly, get the person's attention, speak slowly, and avoid overemphasizing his or her lip movement. An interpreter can facilitate communication between hearing and deaf persons.

When a hearing-impaired person is arrested, he or she should be provided with an interpreter and advised of constitutional rights with a printed form of the *Miranda* warning.

Case Study Exercises/Essays

1. Assume you are Sergeant Pyle:

    a. Would you discuss the problem with the watch commander?
    b. What could you do to ensure good communication between you and the people you supervise?

2. Assume you are Sergeant French:

    a. How could you develop a trusting relationship with the officers?
    b. What is the reason for your communication problem?
    c. How can you improve the communication between yourself and the officers?

Multiple-Choice Questions (Circle the best answer)

1. A breakdown in communication is an inevitable consequence of:
    a. the natural tendency to be easily distracted.
    b. an inability to properly interpret what is said.
    c. the increasing problem of the short attention span.

2. Interpersonal communication exists at every level of any organization, but is most prevalent at the:
    a. mid-management level.
    b. operational level.
    c. upper-management level.
    d. all of the above

3. According to More, Wegener, and Miller, communication is the lifeblood of the organization because:
    a. it is the process that ties the whole organization together.
    b. everyone must talk the same language in order to communicate.
    c. it is a resource in constant use and abuse.
    d. you can't avoid it.

4. In order for communication to be effective, it must be:
    a. reinforced through repetition.
    b. nurtured by all levels of management from the top down.
    c. inherent.
    d. approached cautiously.

5. One study of first-line supervisors cited in the text showed that they spend the least amount of their communication time communicating with:
    a. other supervisors.
    b. citizens.
    c. superiors.
    d. subordinates.

6. A successful communicator is one who:
    a. is not concerned about personal self-esteem.
    b. looks for someone to blame.
    c. upon realization that he or she has not explained something adequately, will still expect the officer to understand and do the job correctly.
    d. does not have a lot to say because others always understand him or her.

7. The sender of the information determines the relevance and the importance of the information, which is known as:
    a. operational autonomy.
    b. gatekeeping.
    c. channeling.

8. Because of _____, the first-line supervisor is in the position of controlling the amount and the nature of information that enters the information system.
    a. gatekeeping
    b. operational autonomy
    c. channeling

9. The first-line supervisor must be concerned about the _____, as it can prove to be more meaningful than the _____.
    a. context, content
    b. content, context
    c. verbal message, nonverbal message
    d. nonverbal message, verbal message

10. According to More, Wegener, and Miller, first-line supervisors spend _____ percent of their communication time communicating with the officers they supervise.
    a. 40
    b. 55
    c. 60
    d. 72

11. When the sender communicates without expecting or receiving feedback from the recipient, he or she is demonstrating:
    a. channeling.
    b. one-way communication.
    c. two-way communication.
    d. none of the above

12. One-way communication is preferable when:
    a.   feedback is required immediately.
    b.   orderliness is insignificant.
    c.   compliance is imperative.
    d.   all of the above

13. Two-way communication requires less planning due to:
    a.   the opportunity for feedback and ability to clarify the issues.
    b.   the error rate for decoding.
    c.   requiring more planning due to so many variables.
    d.   the need for less understanding.

14. The advantages to two-way communication may include:
    a.   improved accuracy and greater understanding.
    b.   no sharing of authority and responsibility.
    c.   less acknowledgment of the importance of communicating.
    d.   no recognition of the fact that subordinates need to know what is expected.

15. Supervisors who use jargon:
    a.   may communicate that officers may treat the people they "label" differently and not in accordance with their constitutional rights.
    b.   may cloud communication.
    c.   may exclude some officers from discussion.
    d.   all of the above

16. There are a number of ways of overcoming communication barriers, including all but which of the following?
    a.   use of one-way communication to reduce the "noise" created by discussion
    b.   continual use of face-to-face communication
    c.   repetition of communication as needed
    d.   constant use of direct and simple language

17. The foundation for real two-way communication occurs when the subordinates accept a supervisor as someone who:
    a.   supports and assists.
    b.   forces, demands, and orders.
    c.   has a job to do that requires orders and demands to be met.
    d.   has a job to do and cannot be their friend.

18. In a real working relationship where there is true commitment from subordinates, there will be:
    a.   no sharing of power.
    b.   mutual respect but no genuine acceptance of one another.
    c.   feelings of trust but not mutual respect.
    d.   genuine acceptance of each other.

19. A supervisor should view each officer as a member of a team by:
    a.   making personality judgements.
    b.   stressing strengths.
    c.   focusing on weaknesses.
    d.   the way the officer relates items of interest about the other officers.

20. A supervisor must convey to each employee that:
    a. he or she makes decisions based on upper-management instructions.
    b. there is no room for flexibility in decisions based on employees' opinions.
    c. he or she is willing to accept the ambiguity of situations because the positive results usually exceed the errors that will occur.
    d. a work environment where subordinates follow without questioning is of primary importance.

21. Spoken communication, in contrast to written communication:
    a. reinforces supportive relationships.
    b. creates an atmosphere characterized by a lack of trust and confidence.
    c. is less reliable due to the greater chance of misinterpretation and should be avoided.
    d. is not recommended.

22. When feedback is provided, it should be:
    a. descriptive and judgmental.
    b. instructive or corrective.
    c. given immediately regardless of circumstances to have impact.
    d. selective but not limited to the issue at hand.

23. According to Albert Mehrabian, the three components of a message that contribute to the communication process in terms of impact are:
    a. 7% actual words, 38% the way it is said, 55% nonverbal.
    b. 40% actual words, 10% the way it is said, 50% nonverbal.
    c. 32% actual words, 38% the way it is said, 30% nonverbal.

24. Body language includes:
    a. posture, words, facial expressions, eye contact, body tension.
    b. posture, facial expressions, eye contact.
    c. body tension, positioning, attention.
    d. eye contact, facial expressions, words.

25. Nonverbal communication is used primarily to convey:
    a. emotions.
    b. desires.
    c. preferences.
    d. all of the above

26. Paralanguage refers to:
    a. tactile communication.
    b. psychic communication.
    c. communication through voice inflections.
    d. written communication.

27. Effective eye contact can be used to:
    a. display aloofness and initiate feedback.
    b. show a lack of confidence, anxiety, and aloofness.
    c. reinforce feedback, solicit or suppress the transmission of a message, and support communication.

True or False Questions

F   1. The need for good communication skills has become increasingly important as the tasks performed have become easier to accomplish.

F   2. Effective communication means getting the meaning across; therefore, a good communicator goes into great detail so there is a lengthy explanation.

T   3. Effective communication involves the transmission of a message and the recipient correctly interpreting the message.

T   4. When goals are compatible there is a greater possibility that a message will be interpreted accurately.

T   5. The recipient of information reacts to a message based on experiences, knowledge, viewpoints, and frame of reference.

T   6. Barriers to communication can include concern about one's knowledge of the subject as well as the probability of being looked upon with displeasure.

T   7. A supervisor can obtain sound feedback only when there is reason for officers to dispel fears and concerns that impede or impair two-way communication.

T   8. A supportive relationship is in which the subordinate is allowed to influence the supervisor.

T   9. Listening is an active process that includes one's intellectual capacity of comprehension and evaluation.

T   10. Successful listeners should strive to keep an open mind and be fully cognizant of their own biases and preconceptions.

T   11. As a good listener, a supervisor must respond intellectually rather than emotionally.

F   12. A good listener waits until the sender completes a message before responding, suspending judgment, which is polite but has little or no effect on misinterpretation.

F   13. A supervisor can improve learning effectiveness by giving undivided attention to the speaker, attempting to listen emotionally, and adjusting to the sender's message

T   14. An effective supervisor recognizes that body language is an important element in the communication process.

F   15. Diversity training is not a component of intercultural communication.

F   16. *Proxemics* refers to the nonverbal communication conveyed through voice pitch, volume, and inflection.

Chapter 4
Motivation—
A Prerequisite for Success

Learning Objectives

1. Describe the *motivation cycle*.

2. Define *motivation*.

3. Identify the elements of a motivational plan.

4. Compare *physiological needs* with *security needs*.

5. List items indicating a strong esteem need.

6. Describe how an officer can become self-actualized.

7. Compare *satisfiers* and *dissatisfiers*.

8. Describe Theory X and Theory Y.

9. Identify the four basic assumptions that underpin the expectancy theory.

10. Define the term *valence*.

11 Describe the theory of sensitivity.

12. Describe the concept of *psychological success*.

Key Concepts

achievement-motivation program
behavior modification
dissatisfiers
ends
esteem needs
expectancy motivational model
expectancy theory
facet feelings
global feelings
human behavior
hygiene
job satisfaction
means

motivation cycle
motivators
physiological needs
positive reinforcement
psychological success
satisfiers
security needs
self-actualized needs
sensitivity
social needs
Theory X—Theory Y
valence

Chapter Summary

I. Why Officers Work

Determining basic human needs is fundamental to understanding human behavior. Human behavior doesn't just happen—it is caused. Behavior follows a pattern showing that:

1.   A need will mobilize the energy to reach an acceptable goal.
2.   As the need increases in intensity, goal attainment becomes emphasized by the individual.
3.   As the need increases, behavior will follow, which hopefully will allow the individual to attain the goal.

A. *Motivation cycle.* Motivation is a continuous process consisting of three specific steps:

1.   *Need.* An individual experiences a need caused by external or internal forces and those forces become mobilized.
2.   *Responding Behavior*. A responding behavior occurs, and energy intensifies and satisfaction occurs.
3.   *Goal.* A goal is reached.

An individual's motivation depends on two factors: the strength of the need and the belief that a certain action will lead to need satisfaction. The intensity of an individual's motivation depends on perception of the real value of the goal.

A supervisor has a direct responsibility to motivate employees and to provide a work environment leading to officer satisfaction. He or she must create conditions to maximize the productivity of officers while department goals are achieved. A supervisor should create an atmosphere of consistency in style in which most officers become self-motivated. Toward these ends, the supervisor should develop an achievement-motivation program.

II. Needs-Based Motivation

Abraham Maslow's theory on the **hierarchy of needs** (see Figure 4.4) is one of the most widespread motivational theories in use. He stated that people's needs were complex and hierarchical, and that the best individuals (purportedly one percent of the population) are self-actualized. Maslow believed that a human being constantly wants something. As soon as one desire is satisfied, another takes its place.

A. *Physiological Needs.* The strongest and most fundamental needs that sustain life, i.e., food, shelter, sex, air, water, and sleep. Deciding the degree to which officers are motivated by physiological needs is important for a supervisor. Concentrating on these needs for motivation is to concentrate on financial rewards.

B. *Security Needs.* This is primarily the need for reasonable order and stability with freedom from anxiety and insecurity.

Supervisors must realize that some officers enter police work because government agencies provide a secure and stable job. These officers want stability and predictability above all else. Security-minded officers want everything in black and white. Management that wants to meet security needs can emphasize traditional union demands and limit complex problem-solving situations or any type of risk taking.

Management must identify the supervisor's need for security as well. A supervisor driven by security needs will be well organized, rigid, and will strive above all else to please and placate the higher chain of command. This supervisor may ignore the needs of the subordinates and use manipulation when necessary. He or she often believes that subordinates have no need to control their own lives.

Individuals should examine their own security needs through the following questions:

1. How far would you go to cover up personal mistakes?
2. Would you cover up mistakes made by supervisors?
3. Would you do anything just to get promoted?
4. Do you always agree with the boss just because that person is the boss?

C. *Social Needs*. An individual needs to have affiliation with others, a place in the group. If social needs are not fulfilled by the organization, an officer will often respond by excessive use of sick time and low productivity.

When a supervisor identifies that the social needs are the motivating needs, the supervisor should promote social interaction for those officers. This can be done through activities such as workout rooms, parties, or sporting events.

Management needs to monitor socially motivated supervisors, because they will emphasize the officers' needs and will ignore the organizational needs. Individuals should examine their own social needs through the following questions:

1. When you become a supervisor can you change roles and lead?
2. How strong is your need to be socially accepted?
3. When you are promoted, can you accept being a part of management?

D. *Esteem Needs*. *Self-esteem* needs include the need for independence, freedom, confidence, and achievement. Needs for *respect* from others include the concepts of recognition, prestige, acceptance, status, and reputation.

Officers who do not feel their esteem needs are being fulfilled by their job will become disgruntled employees. Supervisors should try to recognize their subordinates for a job well done. A supervisor driven by esteem will usually be a good manager because he or she will drive him or herself with deep intensity to be recognized.

E. *Self-Actualization*. This is the stage at which an individual has the need to develop feelings of growth and maturity. He or she becomes increasingly competent and gains a mastery over situations. Motivation is totally internalized and requires no external stimulation. This person usually focuses on being creative and constructive in work situations. When a supervisor recognizes an officer driven by self-actualization, that officer should be included in special assignments that will allow him or her to be creative, such as task forces.

III. Motivation-Hygiene Theory

Frederick Herzberg and his colleagues developed the motivation-hygiene theory, which was based on their study of job satisfaction.

A. *Motivators*. These factors relate to the work itself and revolve around such things as achievement, advancement, recognition, and responsibility. It is primarily the motivators that result in job satisfaction.

B. *Hygiene Factors*. These factors are generally related to work conditions and policies, including such factors as interpersonal relations, salary and benefits, job security, and working conditions. Hygiene factors are generally related to feelings of unhappiness.

IV. Theory X—Theory Y

Theory X—Theory Y, developed by Douglas McGregor, is based on the belief that managers conduct themselves according to their assumptions, generalizations, and hypotheses about human behavior.

Theory X was the prevalent management style for law enforcement in the early days. It is the traditional view of direction and control, which stresses that:

1. The average employee actually dislikes work and will do whatever is necessary to avoid it.
2. If employees dislike work, in order to accomplish the organizational objectives, most employees will have to be coerced, controlled, directed, or threatened with punishment.
3. Security is important to the average employee. This employee has little ambition, and would rather be told what to do.

Theory X places emphasis on control and direction. Procedures are created for providing officers with close supervision and the creation of a means for providing rewards and punishments.

Theory Y appears to apply to the motivation of employees who have developed a social esteem or self-actualization need. Theory Y stresses:

1. Most employees will respond as positively to work as they do to play or rest.
2. Control and direction are not the only techniques to achieve departmental goals. When committed to departmental goals, employees will have self-control and self-direction.
3. Commitment to departmental objectives is a function of the rewards associated with the attainment of objectives.
4. Avoidance of responsibility, an accentuation on security, and limited drive are consequences of experience, not fundamental characteristics of human nature.
5. The ability to exercise a high degree of imagination, ingenuity, and creativity when striving to solve an organizational problem is a talent distributed among the population.
6. With industrial life conditions as they are, the intellectual potential of the average employee is only partially used.

The application of Theory Y reduces the need for external control and relies on other managerial techniques for reaching organizational goals. Supervisors should view officers as assets and develop interpersonal relationships.

V. Expectancy Theory

Victor Vroom documented the expectancy theory.

A. ***Expectancy Theory***. This theory is based on the concept that it is the internal state and external forces impinging upon an individual that will enable the person to act in a specific manner. A worker will be motivated to do what is required of him or her when it will lead to certain desired goals. With this theory, behavior is a product of the vitality of an individual and the environment, and individuals will develop preferences for available objectives. Employees have expectancies about outcomes.

Psychological success. Psychological success as a means to increase self-esteem occurs when a personal challenging goal is set, methods of achieving that goal are set, and the goal is relevant to one's self-concept.

Valence. The strength of an individual's preference that an appropriate outcome will occur.

VI. Sensitivity Theory

This theory is a genetics-behavior-cognitive model of axiomatic motivation. According to two psychologists, human behavior can be separated into two categories based on the purposes of the behavior:

Means. This is indicated when someone performs an act for a useful purpose.

End. This occurs when an individual performs a behavior for no evident reason other than its own purpose.

The researchers postulated that human desire stems from 16 basic desires. They range from abstracts such as honor to social contact, and from bodily wants such as eating or romance, and also more intellectual ambient factors such as idealism and order. Of special interest to the work situation are such fundamental motives as power and independence.

VII. How to Motivate

Supervisors can use behavior modification to influence behavior to meet organizational objectives. Within this framework, officers will continue or repeat behavior with positive consequences and will cease behavior that has negative results.

If a supervisor uses positive reinforcement to modify behavior, it must be done continuously and consistently. Punishment of employees should be a last resort and not a supervisory style. A punishing style of leadership is a negative managerial style that causes employees to react defensively and reduces work productivity. A supervisor should be encouraged to use reinforcement techniques to shape subordinates' behavior. However, reinforcement techniques must be *response-contingent* and utilized thoughtfully and systematically. That is why annual performance reviews usually prove ineffective in changing job behavior.

Case Study Exercises/Essays

1. Assume you are Sergeant Pollard:

    a. What would you do to boost officer motivation?
    b. How would you go about determining the basic need drives of each officer?

2. Assume you are Senior Patrol Officer Hilldebrand's supervisor:

    a. What would you do to make Officer Hilldebrand more productive?
    b. How could you apply the motivation-hygiene theory to Officer Hilldebrand?

Multiple-Choice Questions (Circle the best answer)

1. Which of the following does *not* characterize the pattern that behavior will follow?
    a. A need will mobilize the energy to reach an acceptable goal.
    b. As the need increases in intensity, goal attainment is emphasized by the individual.
    c. As the need increases, behavior will follow that seems to be more promising for goal attainment.
    d. As the need increases beyond a certain level, the employee becomes fixated on the specific need and disregards the ultimate goal.

2. To become an effective supervisor, all of the following are true except:
   a. One must create the conditions that maximize the productivity of the officers.
   b. One must coordinate the officers' efforts so as to achieve departmental goals.
   c. One must recognize that every officer is a unique individual and consequently each individual is stimulated by differing needs.
   d. One must recognize that officers can be motivated by fear.

3. The combination of _____ determines what motivates an officer to act in a certain way in a particular situation.
   a. internal factors and stress
   b. external and internal factors
   c. goals and objectives
   d. external factors and goals

4. A motivated employee is the product of the interaction of the employee with the _____ and the _____ that are generated.
   a. organization, attitudes
   b. work environment, actions
   c. supervisor, actions
   d. work, goals

5. The _____ is a vehicle that aids in the understanding of human behavior and provides an appreciation of interacting forces and resultant behavior.
   a. psychological need
   b. satisfaction cycle
   c. motivation cycle
   d. human needs test

6. An officer who is placed with an organization that really motivates its employees will find all of the below to be true except:
   a. There are identifiable goals.
   b. The culture can readily be identified with.
   c. Tasks are easily accomplished.
   d. Accomplished individuals are rewarded.

7. For many employees, the attainment of _____ is as important as material rewards.
   a. awards
   b. work-related goals
   c. promotion
   d. a global view

8. More, Wegener, and Miller state that what two types of feelings come into play when considering work?
   a. personal and professional
   b. organizational and individual
   c. security and fulfillment
   d. global and facet

9. Within a good workplace, the relationship between each employee and the organization is one of:
   a. reliance.
   b. blind faith.
   c. trust.
   d. acceptance.

10. Based on Herzberg's view of satisfiers and dissatisfiers, hygiene factors:
    a. cannot increase job satisfaction but only affect the amount of job dissatisfaction.
    b. are not related to satisfiers and dissatisfiers.
    c. are directly proportional to job satisfaction.
    d. cannot be measured.

11. When an agency concentrates on physiological needs as a means of motivating officers, they place emphasis on:
    a. interpersonal relationships.
    b. better working conditions.
    c. physical fitness.
    d. extracurricular events.

12. Closely paralleling Theory X is another motivational theory called the:
    a. "do unto others" theory.
    b. "you can lead a horse to water" theory.
    c. necessary evil theory.
    d. carrot and stick theory.

13. Hygiene factors are generally:
    a. long-lived.
    b. short-lived.
    c. not adaptable.
    d. immeasurable.

14. Theory X places a strong emphasis on:
    a. control and direction.
    b. control and relaxation.
    c. direction and relaxation.
    d. control and intimidation.

15. According to More, Wegener, and Miller, when officers are on probation and new to the job, a _____ approach may be more appropriate for supervising them.
    a. Theory X
    b. Theory Y
    c. Theory X—Theory Y

16. Which of the features below is *not* a part of the expectancy theory?
    a. behavior is not determined exclusively by the individual
    b. employees have expectancies about outcomes
    c. effort-performance
    d. performance-input
    e. performance-outcome

17. When reinforcement is used to modify behavior, it must be done:
    a. consistently and continuously.
    b. as needed.
    c. by analyzing each scenario and then making a determination of action and method.
    d. differently on an individual assessment basis.

True or False Questions

F   1. An individual's motivation to act depends on two factors: the strength of the need and the belief that a certain action will lead to need satisfaction.

T   2. A supervisor should strive to create a quality of organizational working life in which most officers become self-motivated.

T   3. As a supervisor, it is your responsibility to develop needs in your officers and, when appropriate, make organizational needs overcome personal needs.

T   4. A federal study showed that neither job security nor short working hours were considered to be of comparable importance to the perceived quality of work.

T   5. Motivation is defined as an action that causes someone's behavior to change.

F   6. An agency in which the conditions are maximized for positive motivation is a department in which one is allowed to be creative and accept a challenge.

T   7. The socially motivated supervisor stresses officers' needs and will ignore organizational needs.

T   8. Supervisors who recognize the importance of esteem needs do everything possible to ensure that officers demonstrate self-confidence.

F   9. A supervisor whose primary drive is esteem will usually be a poor supervisor.

T   10. The self-actualized individual has a need to demonstrate the ability to assume responsibility and involvement at the highest possible level.

T   11. According to McGregor, the worker must be encouraged to develop to his or her highest capacity, acquire knowledge, and acquire skills.

F   12. One factor necessary for motivating employees is for the supervisor to understand that it is the supervisor's perception that counts—not the officer's.

T   13. According to More, Wegener, and Miller, the successful supervisor will concentrate on helping officers to clarify their needs and become aware of how officers perceive those needs.

F   14. Punishment is viewed as the quickest and most effective way of obtaining compliance.

F   15. A punishing style of leadership requires that the supervisor operate continuously from a positive managerial style.

T   16. If reinforcement is used before the desired behavior, it will not shape behavior.

T   17. Reinforcement will modify behavior.

F   18. The key to motivation is the integration of the employee into the organization.

Chapter 5
Leadership—
The Integrative Variable

Learning Objectives

1. Describe the skills required of a first-line supervisor.

2. Define *leadership*.

3. Compare *legitimate* and *expert* power.

4. Identify the limitations of coercive power.

5. List the traits a large police department has identified as qualities required of a good supervisor.

6. Identify the five groups of traits found to be associated with leadership effectiveness.

7. Compare *initiating structure* and *consideration*.

8. Describe the three major components of the contingency model of leadership.

9. Compare *directive* and *participative* leadership behavior.

10. Identify three leadership mistakes.

11. Identify the four critical tasks leaders need to achieve in high-performance operations.

Key Concepts

attributes
authority
coercive power
conceptual skills
consideration
consultative
contingency
directive
expert power
extending power
high control
human skills
initiating structure
leadership continuum

leadership traits
least preferred coworker
legitimate power
low control
moderate control
operational skills
participative
personal relationships
policy
position power
referent power
relationship-oriented leadership
reward power
task-oriented leadership
task structure

Chapter Summary

The authors identify the most important characteristic of a well-managed department as leadership. Management has the responsibility to monitor its supervisors to make sure they are competent and ensure that the officers are not subjected to exploitative leadership by first-line supervisors. A person becoming a supervisor must shift from a focus on operational skills to a greater consideration of human and conceptual skills.

A. *Operational Skills.* These skills involve techniques, methods, and use of equipment.

B. *Human Skills.* Development of the ability to understand why people behave the way they do in order to effectively change, direct, and control behavior. These skills involve motivation, communication, and direction.

C. *Conceptual Skills.* Development of one's knowledge of the overall organization and awareness of how the unit fits into the organization will allow the supervisor to work toward the attainment of organizational goals and increased efficiencies.

Effective leadership contributes to the accomplishment of clearly defined tasks. Four roles are critical to effective leadership:

1.   Direction setter
2.   Change agent
3.   Spokesperson
4.   Coach

D. *Leadership.* The process of influencing group activities toward the achievement of goals.

The first-line supervisor is no longer a doer but a coordinator of others' activities. Supervisors operate from a position of power based on the authority delegated to the supervisor. Supervisory power sources can be positional or personal.

I. Power

According to More, Wegener, and Miller, first-line supervisors can extend power by using the following techniques:

1.   *Persuasion.* A technique in which the supervisor communicates the reason and justification when exerting influence over others.

2.   *Patience.* The technique in which the supervisor shows consideration for the shortcomings and weaknesses of each employee and balances these against an immediate desire to attain objectives.

3.   *Enlightenment.* Development of the ability to accept and value the insights, discernment, and reasoning of subordinates.

4.   *Openness.* The ability to accept officers for who they are now and for what they can become as growth occurs. Requires accurate awareness of goals, values, desires, and intentions.

5.   *Consistency.* Doing what is expected so subordinates will always know where the supervisor is coming from and never feel as though they are being manipulated.

6.   *Integrity.* Striving for control that can only be interpreted as fair, impartial, and non-manipulative. Supervisor exhibits honesty and real concern.

Position and personal power can be further divided into five categories (see Figure 5.3).

A. *Legitimate power.* Power that comes from policy and written directives outlining a supervisor's authority and responsibilities.

B. *Expert power.* Power that comes from the subordinates' knowledge that the supervisor possesses a greater amount of knowledge.

C. *Referent power.* Power that is associated with the leader's personality. Sometimes identified as charisma, it is a quality that makes the supervisor likable.

D. *Coercive power.* Power that is based on fear and the knowledge that the supervisor has the ability to administer some type of punishment.

E. *Reward power.* Power that comes from being able to reward employees in some way.

Power should be viewed with a positive attitude and not abused. Each type of power has its limitations.

II. Theories of Leadership

A. *Trait theory.* Identifies distinguishing qualities or characteristics a person possesses when functioning as an effective leader. One researcher has identified five groups of traits associated with leadership effectiveness: (1) capacity, (2) achievement, (3) responsibility, (4) participation, and (5) status.

B. *Behavioral theory.* Based on Ohio State leadership studies that showed there are two types of leadership behavior:

1.   *Initiating structure.* The leader's behavior in delineating the relationship between him or herself and his or her subordinates and in attempting to establish well-defined patterns of organization, channels of communication, and methods or procedures.

2.   *Consideration.* The leader's behavior indicative of friendship, mutual trust, respect, and warmth in the relationship between the leader and all members.

C. *Contingency model.* Holds that the leader's style must match the demands of the specific situation. Fred Fiedler and associates developed the first contingency model, identifying three factors of importance:

1.   *Position power.* The degree to which the position itself confers on the leader the capacity to get officers to accept and comply with directions.

2.   *Task structure.* The extent to which a task is routine and structured as compared to an ambiguous and poorly defined task. When tasks are carefully defined, it is much easier for a supervisor to control operational duties and officers can be held responsible.

3.   *Personal relationships.* When the relationship between subordinates and a leader can be described as good, the supervisor is in a good position to influence behavior due to trust.

Fiedler identified two basic styles of leadership:

1.   Task-oriented
2.   Relationship-oriented

A leader's power can run from high position power (mutual trust and respect with highly structured tasks) to weak position power (little respect or support with vague tasks).

IV. Leadership Continuum

The relationship between a supervisor and subordinates exists along a continuum. Some researchers limit leadership style to two types (autocratic and democratic), while others identify more (e.g., authoritarian, democratic, laissez-faire, bureaucratic, and charismatic). Regardless of the number of styles, no supervisor sticks to one style. Usually the supervisor adapts his or her style to meet the needs of individual situations.

More, Wegener, and Miller describe three types of leadership behavior when the supervisor wants to influence the behavior of line officers:

1.   *Directive* is when a supervisor exhibits little concern for officers and allows little or no involvement in the decision-making process. A directive leader uses the authority of the position to attain subordinate obedience. This supervisor uses rules and regulations to ensure compliance.

2.   *Consultative* is a leadership style of compromise, when a supervisor shows concern for officers and their needs and also organizational needs. Subordinates are allowed to participate in the decision-making process when it will result in a better decision.

3.   *Participative* is when the supervisor has genuine belief in and respect for subordinates. He or she fosters two-way communication, consulting with subordinates and involving them in the decision-making process. Group involvement is sought and power is shared.

V. Leadership Mistakes

Supervisors work for both management and subordinates. They are responsible not only for telling the officers what to do, but to also coach them when circumstances require it, and to consult with them and join with them to attain objectives. Delegation is essential. The misuse of power by a first-line supervisor may prove useful initially but over a long period can lead to the downfall of a first-line supervisor. It is important to accept individual differences and work with employees to make them the best they can be. Supervisors must be fair.

Case Study Exercises/Essays

1.   Assume you are Sergeant Pike:

   a.   What would you do about the morale problem?
   b.   What would you do to influence the officer's behavior toward the achievement of organizational goals?

2.   Assume you are Sergeant Faxton:

   a.   What would you tell the officers?
   b.   What would you do to improve the performance of the officers you supervise?

Multiple-Choice Questions (Circle the best answer)

1. According to a survey by the Police Foundation:
   a. the chart of the typical police organization is constricted in the middle, where the number of sergeants is outweighed by both line officers below them and the ranks of lieutenant, captain and major above them.
   b. a typical police organization can be diagrammed by an inverted pyramid.
   c. in a typical police organization, sergeants outnumber the combined ranks of lieutenant, captain, and major.

2. Sergeants need to divide their time between doing and managing, which can be referred to as the:
   a. rule of coordination.
   b. rule of balance.
   c. 50 percent rule.

3. Supervisory skills include:
   a. operational, human, and conceptual.
   b. position and power.
   c. direction, delegation, and discussion.
   d. tasks and relationships.

4. Positional power sources include:
   a. expert, reward, coercive.
   b. legitimate, coercive, reward.
   c. referent, expert.
   d. coercive, referent, expert.

5. Personal power sources include:
   a. expert, reward, coercive.
   b. legitimate, coercive, reward.
   c. referent, expert.
   d. coercive, referent, expert.

6. The theories of leadership can be grouped into which three categories?
   a. trait theories, behavioral theories, contingency theories
   b. trait theories, individual theories, group theories
   c. individual theories, behavioral theories, group theories
   d. individual theories, behavioral theories, contingency theories

7. Ralph Stogdill's identified group of traits associated with leadership effectiveness include:
   a. capacity, achievement, and power.
   b. capacity, responsibility, and power.
   c. power, status, and achievement.
   d. status, responsibility, and capacity.

8. The behavioral model identifies two basic types of leadership behavior, which are:
   a. initiating structure and resolution.
   b. resolution and consideration.
   c. consideration and initiating structure.

9. A supervisor who feels comfortable emphasizing consideration is likely to utilize:
    a. one-way communication and emphasize high standards.
    b. one-way communication and show that there is mutual trust.
    c. two-way communication and show respect for officers' ideas.
    d. two-way communication and carefully plan activities.

10. A supervisor who has activities carefully planned and communicated, has deadlines established, and gives instructions is said to be emphasizing:
    a. consideration structure.
    b. resolution structure.
    c. initiating structure.

11. Under the _____, first developed by Fred Fiedler and his associates, the leader's style must match the demands of a specific situation.
    a. leadership continuum
    b. contingency model
    c. behavioral model
    d. consistency model

12. According to Fiedler, there are two basic styles of leadership, which are:
    a. task-oriented, goal-oriented.
    b. goal-oriented, power-oriented.
    c. power-oriented, task-oriented.
    d. relationship-oriented, task-oriented.

13. For the newly appointed supervisor whose influence is limited, the _____ leadership style will be most effective.
    a. goal-oriented
    b. power-oriented
    c. task-oriented
    d. relationship-oriented

14. The interaction of the leadership style, extent of control, and the situational dimension result in a position whereby the relationship-oriented leader is most effective in a _____ situation, and the task-oriented leader is most effective in _____ or _____ situations.
    a. moderate-control, high-control, low-control
    b. high-control, low-control, moderate-control
    c. low-control, moderate-control, high-control

15. In participative management, a manager _____ performs a task alone when it can be accomplished through the efforts of others.
    a. always
    b. seldom
    c. sometimes
    d. never

True or False Questions

F   1. Taking on a leadership position requires first-line supervisors to rely on their established view of themselves and to maintain a reliance on knowledge, methods and techniques that have worked for them in a line position.

T   2. The move to a first-line supervisory position in law enforcement requires greater consideration of human skills.

T   3. The discharge of leadership responsibilities is a demanding role and forces a supervisor to make decisions and control behavior.

F   4. According to More, Wegener, and Miller, leadership is defined as the process of influencing personal activities toward the achievement of goals.

T   5. A knowledgeable supervisor who demonstrates the ability to implement, analyze, evaluate and control situations, and resolve problems is readily accepted.

T   6. The trait approach does not acknowledge the complex interaction between the actions of the leader and the situation.

T   7. The concept of *initiating structure* defines the leader's behavior in delineating the relationship between leader and work group and in endeavoring to establish well-defined patterns of organization, channels of communication, and methods or procedures.

T   8. The concept of *consideration* defines the leader's behavior as being indicative of friendship, mutual trust, respect, and warmth in the relationship between the leader and the work group

F   9. According to Fred Fiedler's theory of leadership, there are four factors of importance.

T   10. The contingency theory incorporates various indices of power that include the leader's official rank and status and the leader's ability to recommend punishments and rewards.

T   11. When tasks are defined, it is much easier for a supervisor to control operational tasks and officers can be held responsible for their actions or inactions.

T   12. According to Fiedler's theory, a structured task is enforceable, while the unstructured task is ambiguous and difficult or impossible to enforce.

T   13. There is no one style of leadership that will be successful all the time with everyone you are supervising.

F   14. Directive leadership advantages are focused on goal attainment and minimal compliance.

T   15. The consultative supervisor shows a concern for officers and their needs as well as organizational needs.

T   16. "The decision involves the personal or work life of an officer and input is sought" demonstrates a consultative style of leadership.

_F_   17. Consultative leadership advantages are focused on minimal compliance and a limited effectiveness in solving problems.

_T_   18. A participative leadership style can *only* be utilized when the supervisor has a genuine belief in and respect for subordinates.

_T_   19. Participative leadership advantages include motivated employees and improved communication.

Chapter 6
Discipline—
An Essential Element of Police Supervision

Learning Objectives

1. Define *discipline.*

2. Compare and contrast the various forms of discipline.

3. Identify the characteristics of an effective disciplinary system.

4. Describe the role of and skills needed by first-line supervisors.

5. Explore the use and abuse of disciplinary action in complex organizations.

6. Understand the keys to effective discipline.

7. Identify the types of disciplinary action available to the first-line supervisor.

8.   Identify the five reaction stages for an individual going through disciplinary action.

9. Develop an appreciation for "firm but fair" disciplinary action.

10. Understand discipline as a multidimensional learning process.

Key Concepts

constructive discharge
constructive discipline
disciplinary action
disciplinary action made to stick
firm, fair, equitable, and lawful disciplinary action
first-line supervisors as disciplinarians
Garrity protection
goal of discipline
"Hot Stove" concept
negative discipline

objectives of the discipline system
peace officer bill of rights
positive discipline
PRICE protocol
progressive discipline
property right
total quality management (TQM)
types of discipline
vicarious liability

Chapter Summary

I. Nature of Discipline

The goal of discipline is to produce desirable behavior. It is considered an essential element of work that ensures overall productivity and an orderly environment. *Discipline* has numerous meanings and uses, but it tends to have negative connotations for many people. In its best context, discipline is considered positive and involves teaching, instruction, training, and remediation. Its purpose is to facilitate corrective action resulting in self-control that is based on the norms and values of the workforce, producing predictable behavior, and organizational efficiency. From this perspective, discipline is a management function.

Sergeants are responsible for nurturing professionalism in officers, and they are also responsible for initiating disciplinary measures when formal action is required. First-line supervisors have to find a balance between self-regulation and organizational control in order to achieve the organization's mission and objectives.

II. Discipline in the Ranks

Each first-line supervisor must develop the skills necessary to influence the behavior of others, to coordinate their activities, and to lead or direct employees in such a way as to gain their respect, confidence, trust, and positive cooperation. Supervision, based on this model, is viewed as an art rather than a science.

Sergeants, as first-line supervisors, are charged with getting police work done through others. They play two distinct roles when it comes to the on-the-job behavior of their subordinates. They are expected to nurture professionalism and be responsible for initiating disciplinary actions that must sometimes be used. To accomplish this goal sergeants use both positive and negative discipline. No matter which method they choose, sergeants try to encourage safe, reasonable, and predictable conduct so their officers are better able to "protect and serve" the community while satisfying their personal needs.

III. Positive Discipline

A. *Positive discipline.* A systematic approach designed to instruct and/or guide employees so that they become loyal, dedicated, responsible, and productive employees.

First-line supervisors should strive to create an environment in which self-discipline is rewarded and imposed discipline is held to a minimum. Effective supervisors help to keep subordinates interested in their jobs and satisfied with working conditions. They must be multidimensional, fulfilling a variety of roles, accentuating the positive and cultivating employee self-worth. Money and other material rewards are very powerful, but recognition that is genuine can have an even greater impact on job-related behavior.

To be effective, a supervisor needs to develop the ability to criticize the *work* the employee does and not the employee. Once certain parameters for accepted behavior are internalized, they serve as a basis for self-control. When employees learn the job and know the standards on which they are judged, they will gain a great deal of self-confidence and personal security.

Total quality management (TQM) empowers employees to create a positive, performance-oriented culture and employee commitment. First-line supervisors must be facilitators in this participative approach.

The authors state that a supervisor can guarantee an improvement in performance through the **PRICE Protocol**, which is:

1. **Pinpoint.** Identify performance problems that must be addressed.
2. **Record.** Document the current performance level of those having problems.
3. **Involve.** Involve officers in determining the best way to deal with problems, the coaching strategies to be used, and how the supervisor will monitor the progress and the rewards or punishments that will occur based on the success or failure of the corrective process.
4. **Coach.** Carry out the agreed-upon coaching strategies by observing and offering timely advice, encouragement, positive reinforcement, and retraining.
5. **Evaluate.** Evaluate and provide feedback on a continuous basis to decide whether the goals of the PRICE protocol have been achieved.

IV. Negative Discipline

A. *Negative discipline.* Discipline that is based on the use of punishment rather than rewards.

In police organizations, supervisors spend a great deal of time and energy coping with marginal employees. When all else fails, sergeants are forced to rely on the imposition of negative discipline to deal with both deviant and marginal personnel. The sergeant must:

1. Identify weaknesses or deficiencies, failures or overt behaviors that require corrective action.
2. Analyze all the factors to assess appropriate action.
3. Initiate and possibly carry out the disciplinary action.
4. Document the case as to cause, analysis, action, and appropriateness.

Sergeants must act reasonably, decisively, and promptly to resolve discipline problems. They have to consider the needs of the employee, the department, the law enforcement profession, and the community. They should strive for constructive discipline that is firm, fair, and impartial. Discipline should not be randomly applied. Sergeants must recognize the needs of their subordinates in order to avoid job dissatisfaction, interpersonal conflicts, poor performance, discipline problems and high turnover rates.

IV. Keys to Effective Discipline

Good disciplinary systems do not come about by accident, but rather by being carefully designed by management. They include the following characteristics:

1. Proper assignment of personnel to a job of their interest, skill, and training.
2. Necessary and reasonable job-related policies, procedures, rules, and regulations to meet employee needs and accomplish the department's goals and objectives.
3. Effective communication regarding performance and acceptable behavior, along with explanations of consequences if not followed.
4. Continuous review, evaluation, and appraisal of personnel.
5. Consistent, fair, and equitable enforcement of all policies, procedures, rules, and regulations.
6. Mutually acceptable disciplinary procedures based on the "due process" model.
7. A formal appeals procedure designed to ensure fairness of all disciplinary actions and serve as a check and balance on the imposition of punitive sanctions.

Two distinct objectives of disciplinary actions are: (1) to reform the individual offender, and (2) to deter others who may have been influenced by the incident. Sergeants must review which penalites are available, feasible, and appropriate in each circumstance. There is no place for anger, revenge, or retribution in the discipline process. It is illegal for a supervisor to misuse power or harass an employee. The imposition of discipline without just cause is viewed as an unconscionable and unacceptable abuse of authority.

Effective disciplinarians are proactive as well as reactive. Good supervisors know the keys to effective discipline are:

1. Don't be a discipline ostrich—don't overlook discipline problems.
2. Be a "Caesar's wife"—all of the sergeant's behavior should be above reproach.
3. Practice the "Hot Stove" rule—discipline should be immediate, based on known rules, consistent, and impersonal.
4. Never lose control.
5. Be instructive.
6. Be firm but fair.
7. Stay out of the employee's private life.
8. State rules/regulations in a positive manner.

9.   Don't be a disciplinary magician—don't make up rules as you go along.
10. Be precise—comply with labor laws, collective bargaining agreements, and civil service regulations. Follow procedures and document actions.

Good supervisors also understand that individuals involved in a disciplinary action may react with denial, anger, bargaining, depression, and acceptance. A good supervisor allows the officer to experience and progress through each of the reaction stages.

V. The Hot Stove Revisited

Douglas McGregor compared an organization's disciplinary system to a red-hot stove. When you touch a red-hot stove, the discipline is immediate, predictable, consistent, and totally impersonal. Under McGregor's theory, the stove not only serves as a deterrent against whom it is applied, but will also train other employees about what the organization will not accept. Telling employees what is expected of them and explaining the negative consequences they may face is an absolute requirement for effective discipline in law enforcement.

VI. Firm but Fair Disciplinary Action

Sergeants play a key role in the police discipline system and have tremendous influence on the process. Firm and fair discipline depends on four critical factors:

1.   Quality of the personnel being recruited by the department.
2.   The effectiveness of the promotion system.
3.   The training given to newly promoted sergeants.
4.   The support that first-line supervisors receive from their superiors.

The decision to use discipline should be made with care. Most departments use a progressive discipline system that provides for increases in punishment for each subsequent offense:

1.   Informal discussion
2.   Oral warning
3.   Written reprimand
4.   Final written warning
5.   Transfer
6.   Suspension
7.   Demotion
8.   Discharge

Progressive discipline uses the belief that the punishment should fit the crime. However, it is not the answer to every problem. It is merely a tool. It will not work with some employee personalities. If the decision to fire an employee is made, it is able to be accomplished through the progressive discipline system. The goal of discipline is to redirect an employee's negative behavior and salvage the employee.

Discipline can be used to promote efficiency and increase job productivity. How the supervisor carries it out will determine the liability the department will incur if the discipline is challenged as an unfair labor practice.

VII. Making the Disciplinary Action Stick

Disciplinary action can be a tool to promote efficiency, effectiveness, and productivity. Reasonable disciplinary action can be made to stick if it is fair and if first-line supervisors learn to avoid certain **mistakes**:

1. No specific misconduct or violation of policy determined.
2. Insufficient warning that the employee's performance or misconduct is unacceptable.
3. No positive evidence to support the charges against the employee.
4. Supervisor demonstrates real or perceived favoritism or discrimination toward employees.
5. No documentation kept of warnings or reprimands.
6. Punishment is severe or excessive.
7. No concern for just cause and procedural due process.

When discipline is not maintained within a department or treated indifferently by supervisors or managers, the quality of service delivered to the community is lowered and the integrity of the profession suffers.

VIII. Personal and Vicarious Liability

Employers and supervisors can be subject to civil action in the form of monetary and/or injunctive relief if it is found that the department has fallen short in certain obligations:

1. Negligent or wrongful acts of the employees
2. Failure to train
3. Failure to supervise
4. Failure to discipline

Case Study Exercises/Essays

1. PSO Jane Roberts is a rookie officer who just finished her probationary period. Roberts was assigned to FTO Tibbetts who has been known to be a ladies man. One day you intervene in an argument between the two officers. It turns out that Roberts is pregnant and the father is Tibbetts.

   Roberts is blaming you, her sergeant, for placing her with Tibbetts during her training. She also says that a lawyer friend of hers is going to help her get worker's compensation because she got pregnant on the job. Assume you are the officer in charge:

   a. Who is at fault in this case?
   b. What mistakes were made from the beginning and how can future occurrences like this be prevented?

2. Officer Hugh Davis has been a police officer for 15 years and is also one of your best friends. You are now his supervisor and have noticed him having problems with his anger. You have discussed this problem with Davis several times and he agreed to seek counseling. Davis has now had charges for police brutality filed against him. You do not believe Davis has gotten help for his anger and you know that one person was fired a year ago for a similar problem. Now internal affairs wants to see you and Davis's evaluations for the last couple of years. Assume you are Davis's friend and supervisor:

   a. What would you say to internal affairs?
   b. What could you do to try to help Davis?
   c. Do you think Davis has a chance of keeping his job?

Multiple-Choice Questions (Circle the best answer)

1. Discipline is:
   a. an adversarial process.
   b. a tool for achieving shared purpose and goal-oriented behavior.
   c. a means of teaching, training, and remediation.
   d. all of the above

2. Every first-line supervisor should strive to create an environment in which:
   a. sanctions are relied on for results.
   b. external or imposed discipline is held to an absolute minimum.
   c. an employee's sense of competence, craftsmanship, and pride is cultivated through discipline.
   d. none of the above

3. _____ are among the most powerful motivators at the disposal of the first-line supervisor.
   a. Disciplinary actions
   b. Shift assignments
   c. Commendations and citations

4. _____ are two of the factors mentioned in the text that create natural parameters for accepted and expected behavior in a given organization.
   a. Rules and regulations
   b. Effective supervision and discipline
   c. Technical expertise and discipline
   d. Camaraderie and technical expertise

5. According to More, Wegener, and Miller, _____ and _____ come with the stripes.
   a. power, authority
   b. respect, power
   c. problem solving, counseling
   d. power, discipline

6. Police officers have emotional job-related security needs, including all of the following *except* the:
   a. need to know exactly what management expects as to work performance and conduct
   b. need for regular feedback from management concerning job performance
   c. need to be treated fairly and impartially by those in management
   d. none of the above

7. According to Peters and Waterman, based on the "people orientation" of contemporary management theory, there is no place for _____ in the disciplinary process.
   a. friendship
   b. guilt
   c. anger
   d. reform

8. The misuse of power by the first-line supervisor does all but which of the following?
   a. destroys the sergeant's credibility
   b. enhances legitimate authority over subordinates
   c. undermines the sergeant's effectiveness
   d. subjects management to ridicule, charges of unfair labor practices, political repercussions, and civil suits

9. Disciplinary action should be:
    a. proactive.
    b. reactive.
    c. both proactive and reactive.

10. According to the "Hot Stove" rule, employees learn quickly because discipline is all but which of the following?
    a. immediate.
    b. predictable.
    c. consistent.
    d. personal.

11. Whether the discipline is firm and fair will depend on critical factors that include all but which of the following?
    a. the quality of the personnel being recruited by the department
    b. the accountability of the management system
    c. the training given to newly promoted sergeants
    d. the support that first-line supervisors receive from their superiors.

12. Effective disciplinary action is always:
    a. based on just cause.
    b. appropriate to the offense and the needs of the offender.
    c. progressively more severe if the subordinate fails to change errant, disruptive, deviant behavior.
    d. all of the above

13. Discipline that is based on the use of punishment rather than rewards is:
    a. positive discipline.
    b. negative discipline.
    c. retributive discipline.
    d. penal discipline.

True or False Questions

1. Discipline is the essential element in work that ensures overall productivity and an orderly environment.

2. Discipline may be used to produce a shared sense of purpose and common goal-oriented behavior.

3. First-line supervisors are expected to nurture professionalism in the employee.

4. According to More, Wegener, and Miller, it is the first-line supervisor who will determine the success or failure of the police department in achieving its mission, goals, and objectives.

5. According to O.W. Wilson, positive discipline manifests itself in the officer's willingness to conform and participate in self-restraint based on professional dedication or a personal commitment to the ethos of the police department.

6. Disciplinary action is inherently punitive and used to regulate work-related behavior.

7. Sergeants are expected to increase the employee's productivity through negative discipline.

_T_   8. It is the first-line supervisor's responsibility to identify the weaknesses, deficiencies, failures, or overt behavior of subordinates.

_T_   9. Inconsistency and favoritism in disciplining subordinates will have an adverse, potentially destructive effect on employee productivity.

_F_   10. A sergeant's actions must be legal, reasonable, inconsistent, and timely.

_T_   11. If a sergeant misunderstands the nature of the job or lacks rudimentary leadership skills, the potential for abuse of the disciplinary apparatus is great.

_T_   12. The accused employee is presumed innocent until proven guilty and the burden of proof is on those involved in direct supervisory management.

_T_   13. First-line supervisors have a duty to act in the best interests of all of the following: the employee, the department, the law enforcement profession, and the community at large.

_T_   14. Supervisory personnel who bend or break the rules promote disruptive and deviant behavior by others in the workforce.

_T_   15. One key to success as a disciplinarian is to ensure that all employees know and fully understand the department's policies, procedures, rules, and regulations.

_V_   16. Failure to sustain a disciplinary action against an employee puts the supervisor at risk for a subsequent civil suit.

_F_   17. When a person going through the process of a disciplinary action exhibits anger or disrespectful behavior, immediate suspension should occur.

Chapter 7
Performance Appraisal—
The Key to Police Personnel Development

Learning Objectives

1. Define the term *labor-intensive*.

2. Explore the function of performance appraisal.

3. Identify the characteristics of objective performance appraisals.

4. List the steps in the performance evaluation process.

5. Describe the role and responsibilities of each actor in the performance evaluation process.

6. Examine the specific role of the police sergeant in performance evaluation.

7. Compare and contrast selected methods used to appraise on-the-job performance.

8. Describe errors that skew performance evaluations.

9. Describe both the purpose of and dynamics involved in the appraisal interview.

10. Define *remediation* and *follow-up* in terms of the performance evaluation process.

11. Discuss the concepts of *validity* and *reliability* in performance appraisal.

12. Explore performance evaluation in the context of community-oriented policing.

13. Examine the emergence of trends related to appraising the performance of first-line police supervisors.

Key Concepts

appraisal interview
community-oriented policing
cycle of evaluation
employee assistance program (EAP)
errors
evaluating supervisor performance
evaluation interview
evaluative methods
follow-up
frequency of evaluation
goals and objectives
institutional support
Neighborhood-Oriented Policing (NOP)

objectivity, validity, reliability
objective assessment
participation and empowerment
performance appraisal
performance evaluation
performance measures
personnel and productivity
personnel development
remediation
roles and responsibilities
sources of error
supervisor's leading role

Chapter Summary

I. Performance Appraisal

First-line supervisors' responsibilities include preparing performance evaluations, but few receive proper training in how to do it. Police managers recognize that quality of service is likely to revolve around the recruitment and selection of personnel, and that important officer qualities include intelligence, ability, skill, experience, integrity, and dedication.

Management theorists believe that objective and fair performance appraisal systems enrich the relationship between the supervisor and the subordinate. Many human resource managers strongly believe that the real objective that a performance appraisal should meet is to inform employees about the quality of their work so they might strive to improve their own performance.

A supervisor must know who is responsible for what and how the job is done. Performance appraisals should have certain characteristics:

1. Job-centered with focus on specific tasks.
2. Clear and simply stated.
3. Observable and objective.
4. Target actual on-the-job performance.
5. Measurable in terms of predetermined performance standards.

The four universal aspects of performance appraisals are:

1. A performance goal, standard, or plan.
2. Measurement of job-related performance.
3. Comparison of employee performance with the goal, standard, or plan.
4. The use of corrective action.

Performance appraisals have been determined to be necessary by management to:

1. Allocate resources.
2. Reward competent employees.
3. Provide valuable feedback to workers.
4. Maintain fair relationships and open communication.

Officers, supervisors, and managers have distinct roles in the appraisal system, but unity of purpose is very important.

II. Frequency of Evaluation

Formal evaluations should be performed on a schedule. If a supervisor evaluates an officer too frequently, the evaluator runs the risk of placing too much emphasis on normal day-to-day situations. If a superior evaluates an officer too infrequently, the risk is not remembering the critical incidents.

Probationary periods are valuable tools for quality control in the personnel screening process; however, there must be careful, consistent, and objective evaluations of the employee's on-the-job performance. Objective, thorough, and frequent performance appraisals ensure quality police service, protect the public, and promote professionalism.

III. The Sergeant's Role

The first-line supervisor is the person usually responsible for the on-the-job performance evaluation of line personnel. Sergeants must realize that assessing a subordinate's job performance goes with the job and that how well it is done will depend on them. Being a good evaluator requires:

1. Natural talent
2. Knowledge
3. Acquisition of special skills

Supervisors also require institutional support. They must be given management's support and be empowered with the authority to do a meaningful evaluation of subordinates. Management must properly train the supervisor and give access to needed departmental resources. When performance evaluations lack relevance, they can destroy the supervisor's morale and undermine the credibility of management.

Effective supervisors accept performance appraisals as a challenge and feel that it is worth taking risks because it offers them an opportunity to provide substance and form to the agency's resources. They help to eliminate incompetent personnel and offer positive reinforcement to personnel who deserve it.

The three common objectives of personnel evaluations are:

1. **Objective assessment.** To assess each employee's contribution to the organization.
2. **Appraisal interview.** To give employees valuable feedback concerning their performance.
3. **Remediation.** To develop a mutually acceptable plan for correcting any problems.

IV. Methods of Appraisal

The text outlines a few of the more important methods of appraisal.

A. ***Graphic Rating Scale.*** This is done on a line scale to which the evaluator indicates the degree to which the person possesses the trait. The graphic scale ranges on a continuum from negative to positive. The advantages of this rating scale are that it is simple to design and construct, easy to use, easy to interpret, and employees can be compared based on a composite score. The disadvantages of this rating scale are rigidity, rater error, and the possibility of intentional manipulation skewing the results. — LT. Harris

B. ***Critical Incident Method.*** Involves identifying, classifying, and recording significant employee behaviors, whether favorable or unfavorable. It requires three basic steps:

1. Accurate collection and documentation of the incidents.
2. Breaking the information down into categories of significant job behaviors.
3. Providing the evaluator with a list of categories and a form on which to record an analysis.

C. ***Behaviorally Anchored Rating Scales.*** BARS are gaining popularity in the police area. This method focuses on specific on-the-job activities rather than personal traits. Sample statements are used to describe unacceptable, average, and excellent performance in representative incidents. The supervisor evaluates definite, observable, and measurable job behavior, choosing a numerical designation and incorporating these in a matrix configuration. While quite complex, adequate training and effective use make for a win-win situation.

D. ***Management by Objectives.*** MBO is a process designed to convert goals and objectives into specific programs. The employee and the first-line supervisor get together to map out future goals and objectives, measures of achievement, and time frames. On the next evaluation, the employee is evaluated on the identified measures of achievement on which the employee and supervisor previously agreed.

V. The Human Factor

The integrity of the personnel assessment process is directly linked to the ability and skill of the sergeant. A first-line supervisor must be an impartial evaluator. In performance evaluations there are opportunities for *errors*, which refer to influences that affect perceptions and interfere with objective assessment. Supervisors can be trained to recognize common errors in order to find ways to avoid them.

A. ***Error of leniency***. This is the most common error and involves the human tendency to give people the benefit of the doubt. This usually occurs due to supervisors wanting to be popular and to avoid interpersonal conflicts. It also protects one's ego from criticism. The error of leniency undermines the objectivity of the performance assessment process. Effective supervisors have to guard against allowing personal considerations to affect their evaluation of a subordinate.

B. ***Error of central tendency***. This error places the employees into an artificial category of "average." The error of central tendency affords the supervisor a process that makes him or her feel safe and will meet with the least amount of resistance by the employees. This error penalizes the highly motivated employee while it rewards the marginal employee. This error destroys the credibility of the evaluation process and seriously affects employee morale.

C. ***Error of the halo effect***. This frequent error occurs when a supervisor allows one significant event or characteristic to be the basis for the overall rating of the employee. The evaluator then uses selective perception to justify the initial assessment.

The *error of related traits* occurs when the evaluator assumes that an employee who exhibits one strength will automatically possess others.

The *error of overweighting* is when the supervisor is unduly influenced by a critical incident (positive or negative) near the end of the evaluation period.

D. ***Error of bias***. This error involves personal bias and is usually based on the supervisor's norms, values, prejudices, and operational stereotypes. Factors such as race, sex, sexual preference, creed, appearance, and lifestyle may affect the evaluation—whether intentionally or unintentionally. Supervisors are evaluating the person rather than the on-the-job performance. Even when a supervisor does not like the individual employee, the evaluation should be fair and based on objective data.

E. ***Contrast error***. This error occurs when supervisors judge employees based on their own expectations and aspirations rather than actual job performance. This emotion-based evaluation is subjective. If detected by the employees, this error usually forces employees to guess what qualities or traits the supervisor is looking for and to gain approval through win-at-all-cost competitiveness or outright deception.

F. ***Recency Error***. The error of recency occurs when too much weight is placed on the employee's behavior immediately prior to the rating evaluation. Generally, recency error results in a higher rating than actually deserved by the subordinate. Most subordinates are aware of evaluation dates and are likely to increase their work performance in anticipation of evaluation.

Supervisors who are properly trained in the evaluation process are the keys to efficiency, effectiveness, and productivity in police work.

VI. The Validity and Reliability of Performance Appraisal

The objective of the performance assessment is to develop an accurate profile that will determine the competency of the personnel. It should identify individual capabilities and the employee's worth to the organization. Therefore, the validity and reliability of the evaluation are critical to the success of the process.

A. A *valid* performance appraisal should accurately measure the traits, applied problem solving, or goal attainment of the individual. The appraisal itself is an assessment of the degree to which a very specific accomplishment is related to a clearly stated performance standard. With a valid evaluation process, the measuring device will arrive at essentially the same result by any evaluator.

B. A *reliable* appraisal process measures appropriate job-related performance accurately and consistently each time it is used. This appraisal will not be biased by errors of the rater, manipulation by the employee, flaws in the measuring device, or constraints of time or place.

To overcome problems with a performance appraisal, the following actions may help add to the reliability of the process:

1. Develop clear policies, procedures, rules, and regulations to govern the performance evaluation process.
2. Select a simple but valid performance appraisal instrument.
3. Train supervisors in gathering and interpreting objective evaluative data.
4. Active participation by the person being evaluated in all aspects of performance assessment.
5. A commitment by management to make personnel decisions on the data obtained from the formal performance appraisals.

VII. The Evaluation Interview

After completion of the evaluation, the results and recommendations should be communicated to the employee as soon as possible. The evaluation interview can be beneficial to the employee, the sergeant, and the organization.

The performance appraisal interview should be a forum for a positive face-to-face meeting between supervisor and subordinate. It should result in collaborative problem solving and mutual goal setting. For it to be productive, the sergeant must be open and honest with the subordinate while still being helpful and supportive. The employee must be receptive and willing to cooperate by taking direction from the supervisor. The appraisal interview should explore the employee's strengths and weaknesses. It allows the supervisor the opportunity to offer positive reinforcement when appropriate and to address deficiencies and develop a plan to deal with them. The interview should be set up to focus the subordinate's attention on the future. To do this, the sergeant should conduct the interview in the following way:

1. Discuss actual performance in detail, yet be tactful.
2. Emphasize strengths to build on.
3. Promote conforming to acceptable job performance.
4. Stress the opportunities that will allow the subordinate to grow personally while developing professionally.
5. Assist the subordinate in goal-setting with a few specific objectives that can be attained within a reasonable period while considering the available resources.

The interview should involve the following:

1. Evaluating
2. Teaching
3. Coaching
4. Counseling

The success of the interview depends largely on the supervisor's ability to establish rapport, empathize, and communicate effectively with subordinates. The interview should help the subordinate to have an enthusiastic attitude about returning to work and a desire to improve on-the-job performance.

Performance appraisals and interviews must include remediation and follow-up in order to be effective.

VIII. Remediation

A. ***Remediation.*** Using the available resources to correct a personnel problem or remedy a deficiency. Supervisors normally deal with assessment and the appraisal interview, but the sergeant's role in remediation may be less direct. Sergeants usually deal directly with minor deficiencies or performance problems. If the subordinate's performance does not improve, the sergeant is responsible for recommending remediation, possibly through retraining, increasingly severe discipline, or termination from the agency.

Upper management is responsible for resolving serious or persistent performance problems. The sergeant's role then switches to one of advisor and information-gatherer. Employee assistance programs (EAPs) are relatively new programs and play an important role in helping deviant, maladjusted, or marginal personnel who are capable of contributing to the organization. The sergeant can be trained to make preliminary diagnosis of the problem and make a referral to an EAP.

IX. Follow-Up

It is the sergeant's responsibility to monitor the subordinate's progress toward reaching the mutually agreed-upon goals established during the performance interview. Without proper follow-up the performance appraisal becomes meaningless. Appraisal should be a daily activity that becomes documented for the employee periodically as a performance evaluation. Follow-up is designed to motivate personnel and should lead to professional growth and development.

X. Trends in Performance Appraisals

Performance evaluations have become more positive and helpful and less negative or punitive for the subordinate. The supervisor clearly has the responsibility to lead subordinates to better performance, not to rule through fear and intimidation because of their position of authority. Two trends have emerged from an emphasis on participatory management: (1) evaluating officer performance under community policing, and (2) subordinates evaluating supervisor performance.

Traditional performance evaluations are not geared to community-oriented policing. Modification through the following three steps will still allow the process to be effective.

1. Convey reasonable expectations about the content and style of police personnel behavior while reinforcing commitment to the department's mission, values, goals, and objectives.
2. Document the types of incidents that officers are experiencing in their communities and the problem-solving strategies they use.
3. Identify the organizational factors that hinder performance enhancement or the solicitation of ideas for dealing with changing conditions.

While many private enterprises ask employees to rate supervisors, the concept has been slow to develop in policing. Because there is so much that a supervisor does that the subordinate cannot see, theorist Thomas Whetsone believes the appraisal should be only in the area of leadership. He also believes that employees require training on how to evaluate the supervisor if the appraisal is going to offer any credible feedback and that officers should use a standard forced-choice instrument.

In order for the process to work effectively, it must to be structured to remove fear of retaliation and errors such as those discussed earlier. Management's commitment to the concept will go a long way toward sucess in supervisor evaluation. The ultimate goal is self-improvement.

Case Study Exercises/Essays

1. Sergeant Wayne DePriest is in the state highway patrol. He supervises eight other officers in his district. For years the evaluation form has been the same, but a new set of officials is revamping the form to try to improve the quality of work the troopers are doing. Many problems arose under the new system because it was much more in-depth than the others and showed flaws of officers that the other forms did not. This new method began to cause troopers to become very competitive and a lot of "backstabbing" started going on. The number of citizen complaints increased and the officers became much too aggressive. Assume you are Sergeant DePriest:

    a.   How would you use the new evaluation?
    b.   Would you try to change the process or the officers?

2. Sergeant Thorndike is a new officer who has aspirations of becoming a chief of police one day. Sergeant Holleran is retiring and Thorndike will be taking his place. Holleran is well-liked by the officers and has been on the force for 32 years. After being on the job a short time, Thorndike begins to think the officers' past evaluations have been inflated. Thorndike calls all the officers into his office to discuss their performance. After this meeting, the officers file formal complaints against Sergeant Thorndike. Now Thorndike must explain these complaints to his lieutenant. Assume you are Sergeant Thorndike:

    a.   What would you say to the Lieutenant?
    b.   What would you do to help the officers improve using the evaluation process?

Multiple-Choice Questions (Circle the best answer)

1. Many personnel specialists believe that a performance appraisal system should be limited to one objective, which is to:
    a.   inform employees about the quality of their work so they might strive to improve performance.
    b.   show each employee how well the supervisor likes him or her.
    c.   show how effective each officer is as a team player.
    d.   demonstrate what behavior is unacceptable.

2. The most important elements of performance appraisal include all but which of the following characteristics?
    a.   They are job-centered.
    b.   They are clear and simply stated.
    c.   They are objective as well as subjective.
    d.   They are observable.
    e.   They are measurable in terms of a predetermined performance standard.

3. According to More, Wegener, and Miller, a performance appraisal is necessary in order to do all of the following except:
    a.   allocate resources
    b.   reward competent employees
    c.   provide valuable feedback to workers
    d.   determine an officer's right to receive a merit raise and maintain fair relationships and open communication

4. According to More, Wegener, and Miller, under ideal circumstances, police departments should require at least:
    a. two years of probation, with rookie police officers evaluated every six months.
    b. one year of probation, with rookie police officers evaluated every month.
    c. eighteen months of probation, with rookie police officers evaluated every three months.
    d. one year of probation, with rookie police officers evaluated every six months.

5. To be effective, the evaluation process must ultimately include:
    a. assessment.
    b. evaluation.
    c. remediation.
    d. counseling.

6. Methods of appraisal include all but which of the following?
    a. graphic rating scale
    b. critical incident method
    c. BARS
    d. management by objectives
    e. total quality management

7. The advantage of the critical incident method is that:
    a. deals with hypothetical situations
    b. zeroes in only on positive aspects of behavior
    c. is well-suited for the employee counseling aspect of performance assessment

8. When supervisors give the person the benefit of the doubt and evaluate the person higher than the circumstances warrant, they are guilty of the error of:
    a. leniency.
    b. central tendency.
    c. contrast.
    d. bias.

9. According to More, Wegener, and Miller, the most common error in rating police personnel is the error of:
    a. leniency.
    b. central tendency.
    c. contrast.
    d. bias.

10. When supervisors force many employees into an artificial category labeled "average," they are guilty of the error of:
    a. leniency.
    b. central tendency.
    c. contrast.
    d. bias.

11. When the supervisor allows just one outstanding characteristic or critical incident to shape the overall rating, the supervisor is guilty of the:
    a. error of leniency.
    b. error of central tendency.
    c. halo effect.
    d. error of bias.
    e. error of contrast.

12. According to More, Wegener, and Miller, while the exact configuration varies from one department to the next, most formal employee evaluation systems have _____ steps.
    a. three
    b. five
    c. nine
    d. 11

13. When supervisors have a tendency to rate the employees they know and really like much higher than can reasonably be justified by an objective performance assessment, they are guilty of the error of:
    a. leniency.
    b. central tendency.
    c. contrast.
    d. bias.

14. Because much of a supervisor's work is not observed by employees, the supervisor evaluation should focus on:
    a. leadership issues.
    b. personality.
    c. team spirit.
    d. productivity.

15. _____ penalize(s) competent, achievement-oriented employees and reward(s) marginal employees.
    a. Favoritism
    b. Personal politics
    c. Average evaluations
    d. Self-fulfilling prophecies

16. When supervisors tend to judge subordinates in terms of their own expectations and aspirations, they are guilty of the error of:
    a. leniency.
    b. central tendency.
    c. contrast.
    d. bias.

17. The performance appraisal interview benefits:
    a. the employee.
    b. the supervisor.
    c. the agency.
    d. all of the above

18. A performance evaluation that is an accurate measurement of the traits, applied problem solving, or goal acquisition the evaluation purports to measure is said to be:
    a. valid.
    b. reliable.

19. A performance evaluation that is not biased by the idiosyncrasies of the rater, manipulation by the evaluator, flaws in the design of the measuring device, or the constraints of time or place is said to be:
    a. valid.
    b. reliable.

True or False Questions

__T__ 1. Systematic performance appraisal is regarded as the key to employee development and is viewed as the centerpiece of an effective police personnel system.

__T__ 2. The universal aspects of performance appraisal are the use of corrective action as required in a given situation and the measurement of job-related performance.

__T__ 3. Not everyone has the inclination or talent to be a good evaluator.

__T__ 4. Being a good evaluator requires natural talent and acquisition of special skills.

__T__ 5. Influences that distort perceptions and interfere with an objective assessment are the halo effect and the errors of leniency, central tendency, and bias.

__F__ 6. Reliability of performance appraisal is somewhat easy to achieve.

__F__ 7. Institutional support is not essential for a performance appraisal program to be effective.

__F__ 8. Graphic rating scales are tricky performance assessment devices because interpretation is quite difficult.

__T__ 9. A constructive performance assessment interview focuses the subordinate's attention on the future rather than the past.

__F__ 10. The EAP movement assumes it is better to "cut losses" with problem employees than to try to salvage them with costly intervention.

__F__ 11. According to theorist Thomas Whetstone, officers doing supervisor evaluations should remain anonymous so that they can be totally honest without fear of retaliation.

__T__ 12. Clarity and specificity are essential components of MBO.

Chapter 8
Team Building—
Maximizing the Group Process

Learning Objectives

1. Describe the socialization process in a police department.

2. Prepare a short essay describing the relationship between the individual and the group.

3. Compare vertical and horizontal cliques.

4. Identify the characteristics of a random clique.

5. Describe the stages in the group development process.

6. List the elements that constitute norms in a law enforcement agency.

7. Describe how a supervisor can build a winning team.

8. List the ways in which task forces can be advantageous.

9. Describe the manner in which one should conduct a meeting.

Key Concepts

building a winning team
cliques
conducting meetings
collaborate
conform
contribute
controversy and conflict
cooperate
deadly force
effective relationships
formal groups
group development process
group development stages
group norms
group performance
group problem solving
groupthink
horizontal cliques
individual
individual and the group

importance of the individual
informal groups
interaction
isolation
law enforcement norms
loyalty
performance
police culture
preparation
random cliques
resolution
role of the group
silence
size of team
stages of group development
task force
team building
team goals
team meetings
vertical cliques

Chapter Summary

A supervisor must acquire an understanding and working knowledge of group dynamics.

A. *Group*. Consists of two or more people who interact with and influence each other for a common purpose.

Two key factors to group dynamics are:

1.   Interaction
2.   Influence

I. The Individual

Socialization of a police agency is the means by which a new employee is indoctrinated into the organization. The new employee must adjust to the organization—the organization should never adjust to the individual.

The agency will generally require officers to acquire norms, values, and specific behavior developing from:

1.   organizational goals.
2.   approved means utilized to achieve goals.
3.   individual responsibility as defined by the agency.
4.   behavior patterns required as a part of performance.
5.   policies, rules, and regulations that maintain the organization.

The police academy emphasizes conformity and rejects individuality. Then the field training officer system brings the peer value system to the officer. These factors perpetuate the long-standing "us against them" mentality that isolates police from the community. Because of changing demographics and standards of new officers, individuals are not adjusting as they have in the past, and the strong police identity has been weakened. However, the socialization process is still a factor in the development of commitment and loyalty.

II. The Individual and the Group

Supervisors must realize that groups, whether formal or informal, will always exist within an organization. While many officers may work alone day to day, there are benefits to forming groups—such as building a sense of belonging, attachment to the agency, and a sense of stability. The supervisor's primary responsibility is to achieve results through people. The more information a supervisor can develop about the members of the group, the more effective the supervisor can be when working with the group. Groups can be destructive or supportive. Understanding group dynamics will enhance success.

III. Role and Function of the Group

Knowing how a group functions usually leads to more effective problem solving.

A. *Formal Groups.* Created and supported by the organization for the express purpose of fulfilling specific organizational needs or performing special tasks. They are either temporary or permanent depending on the needs of the organization.

B. ***Informal Groups.*** Evolve as a result of the formal organization being unable to meet all social or departmental officer requirements. These groups are rarely sanctioned by the formal organization, and they often cut across organizational lines. These groups can evolve into cliques and break down into three types. Cliques can lead to understanding and hostility.

1. *Vertical Cliques.* Generally occur in one unit of the department, usually between the first-line supervisor and the subordinates. The goal is to humanize the organization and reduce friction between the department and the officers. The supervisor protects the subordinates by disregarding errors and minimizing problems. The officers, in turn, protect the supervisor.

2. *Horizontal Cliques.* Cut across departmental lines and will normally include many first-line supervisors. This clique prefers to work defensively and works most effectively when it is dealing with problems that may weaken one's authority or create some change that is adverse to the members' welfare. Usually more powerful than the vertical clique, it strives to maintain the status quo.

3. *Random Cliques.* Rather than striving for change, its members merely desire to associate with other members of the department. Officers become members for the primary purpose of exchanging information. It is usually the primary source of rumors. The clique can be used to pass on information or as an information source. This group intensifies social relationships within the department.

IV. Group Development Process

A newly organized group passes through six stages:

1.   Orientation
2.   Conflict and challenge
3.   Cohesion
4.   Delusion
5.   Disillusion
6.   Acceptance

As a group forms, the members develop techniques to control the behavior of others. These techniques are called group norms. Norms are unwritten but can be more powerful than organizational rules and regulations. They are powerful because they are backed by the power of the group. They develop through social interaction, and they provide continuity in the work environment, predictability of behavior that leads to a feeling of well-being, and the carrying out of routine procedures without disruption. Law enforcement norms include loyalty, secrecy, danger, deadly force, isolation, and performance.

V. Group Performance

Supervisors must view working with the group as a challenge and should develop a positive attitude toward groups. Groups can have greater productivity because they allow officers to specialize and use their own special skills. They are a tool for bringing resources together to solve problems.

Group cohesiveness is important and generates a great degree of loyalty, identity, acceptance, and conformity. Cohesiveness is enhanced when the group successfully attains its objectives. Although group cohesiveness is a positive factor leading to high productivity, the negative side is the possibility of the group coming together and using its power to resist management.

VI. Building a Winning Team

Team building is a complex process that requires a great deal of leadership and team effort. Supervisors must create an environment that motivates its members to truly function as a team. Effectiveness of the group is influenced by factors such as size, norms, goals, and environment.

Group leaders who are viewed as highly productive show similar characteristics. They:

1. focus continuously on a goal.
2. act as the leader of group activities while participating in the group.
3. control the relationship between the group and other people or units.
4. facilitate assumption of leadership roles when the situation dictates.

A supervisor should try to develop effective and positive personal relationships within a group. Then the supervisor can seek out group members to obtain opinions and open communication. The supervisor should ask questions that deal with problems and not personalities. The larger the team, the more difficult it is to obtain esprit de corps and cohesiveness. The smaller the team, the greater the potential for interaction among its members. It is recommended that teams be kept to around 10 members, and fewer than that when possible.

One of the supervisor's biggest challenges is to create sufficient opportunities for interaction, and officers' time should be scheduled to ensure adequate time for group interaction. Disagreements are normal, and it is important to focus on issues rather than personalities. When controversy occurs, it should be dealt with openly within the group. An effective supervisor should try to be aware of everything that is happening and deal with potential problems. This is best achieved through two-way communication and listening. Conflict or potential conflict should be handled immediately.

VII. Team Goals

The first-line supervisor is responsible for setting goals and directions for the team that are clear and meaningful. Priorities should be set with no room for misinterpretation. It is important that there be openness at all times, and all issues should be handled candidly. This will lead to the development of a cohesive group.

VIII. Group Problem Solving

Group problem solving in police work is typically handled by means of a task force. Task forces are usually temporary, focusing on one subject or problem. The role of the supervisor is to maximize the advantages of group decision making to reach the best possible decision. Advantages of task forces include:

1. Decision making is improved.
2. Greater acceptance of decisions.
3. Coordination is improved.
4. Problems are viewed from a broader perspective.
5. Power is shared.

Task forces are a good training mechanism for teaching officers to make decisions based on a consensus. A task force sets an atmosphere for power sharing.

A supervisor also needs to realize the disadvantages of a task force:

1. Biases of members can be intensified.
2. Excessive influence of individuals with rank or expertise.
3. Domination by individuals within the group.

4.   Diffused responsibility.
5.   Cost in terms of time and money.

IX. Conducting Meetings

Meetings should begin with the establishment of ground rules—setting out the nature, frequency, and goals of the meetings. Consensus is integral to the success of the decision-making process. Supervisors should facilitate interaction and communication. Groupthink is a deliberating style that can be used when consensus is more important than arriving at the best solution.

Case Study Exercises/Essays

1.   Assume you are Sergeant McDonald:

   a.   What types of issues would you discuss at a team meeting?
   b.   How would you get officers to work as a team?

2.   Assume you are Sergeant Cabalar:

   a.   What data would you want the crime prevention specialist to provide?
   b.   What would you discuss at your first team meeting?

Multiple-Choice Questions (Circle the best answer)

1.   Groups that are created to fulfill specific organizational needs or perform special tasks are:
   a.   informal work groups.
   b.   formal work groups.
   c.   cliques
   d.   clubs

2.   Groups that cut across organizational lines and have common interests are:
   a.   informal work groups.
   b.   formal work groups.
   c.   clubs
   d.   cliques

3.   Which clique's goal is to humanize the organization and reduce friction between the department and the officers?
   a.   vertical
   b.   horizontal
   c.   random
   d.   parallel

4.   The _____ clique includes a number of first-line supervisors and functions most effectively when it is dealing with problems that are perceived as weakening one's authority.
   a.   vertical
   b.   horizontal
   c.   random
   d.   parallel

5. The _____ clique assumes a defensive posture and only functions when the situation dictates that it must respond to ensure the status quo.
    a.   vertical
    b.   horizontal
    c.   random
    d.   parallel

6. The stage of group development that is most critical to the success of the group is:
    a.   orientation.
    b.   conflict and challenge.
    c.   cohesion.
    d.   delusion and disillusion.
    e.   acceptance.

7. Which of the following stages occurs when each member of the group has received enough information to accept that the group objective and leadership are legitimate?
    a.   orientation
    b.   conflict and challenge
    c.   cohesion
    d.   delusion and disillusion
    e.   acceptance

8. The stage when the group becomes aware that everything is not moving smoothly and uncertainty enters the picture is:
    a.   orientation.
    b.   conflict.
    c.   cohesion.
    d.   delusion.
    e.   acceptance.

9. The stage when the group fully accepts that they are on a treadmill and are going nowhere is:
    a.   conflict.
    b.   cohesion.
    c.   delusion.
    d.   disillusion.
    e.   acceptance.

10. _____ are techniques that members of a group develop in order to control the behavior of others.
    a.   Rules
    b.   Biases
    c.   Attitudes
    d.   Norms

11. Extensive rules and regulations serve to reinforce this norm, and specific sanctions apply to those who deviate from the expected behavior. Which of the following norms is it?
    a.   Loyalty
    b.   Belonging
    c.   Danger
    d.   Security

12. Which of the following groups is distinguished from other groups because it is usually temporary and focuses attention on one subject or problem?
    a.   committee
    b.   task force
    c.   clique
    d.   union

13. According to the text, which two factors are important to the definition of a group?
    a.   size and competition
    b.   interaction and influence
    c.   belonging and purpose
    d.   members and goals

14. _____ into the police agency is the means by which rookies are transformed from civilian status to productive members of an operating agency.
    a.   Initiation
    b.   Recruitment
    c.   Socialization
    d.   Actualization

15. _____ can be important to the group and is the result of an officer's desire to be a member of the group and the degree of commitment felt by group members.
    a.   Cohesiveness
    b.   Acceptance
    c.   Productivity
    d.   Esprit de corps

16. _____ is not one of the four Cs of team membership
    a.   Contribution
    b.   Collaboration
    c.   Consistency
    d.   Cooperation

True or False Questions

F   1.   Types of informal groups include parallel, vertical, and random.

F   2.   The horizontal clique serves a highly important function by intensifying social relationships within the department.

F   3.   Groups serve as vehicles for decreasing personal relationships because social needs are more easily satisfied.

T   4.   Groups that are cohesive can become an additional problem for first-line supervisors because they possess more power than any one officer.

T   5.   The advantage of a task force is that its final solution will be implemented because of the involvement of a cross section of the department.

T   6. The advantages of a task force include power sharing and viewing problems from a broader perspective.

T   7. Within a police department, both formal and informal groups will always exist.

T   8. A supervisor's roles in team building are facilitator and developer.

T   9. Disadvantages of a task force include: bias of members can be intensified and cost in terms of time and money.

F   10. To maintain authority with a group, the supervisor should avoid any actual personal relationships with the group.

Chapter 9
Change—
Coping with Organizational Life

Learning Objectives

1. Define *change*.

2. Describe what constitutes the process of change.

3. Identify the components of social values.

4. Describe the importance of police unions as a major component of the change process.

5. List the key elements of job satisfaction.

6. Describe the reasons officers accept change.

7. List what employees feel are unpopular decisions.

8. Describe how officers can participate in change.

9. Describe the pitfalls of mandated change.

10. Name the attributes of the police subculture.

Key Concepts

accepting change
ambiguity is created
being knowledgeable
collective bargaining
communication
cultural reasons
discretion is restricted or eliminated
factors fostering change
habits are altered
informal leaders
involvement
job satisfaction

law
mandated change
nature of resistance
need satisfaction
police unions
positive aspects of change
relationships are restricted
resistance to change
social values
unpopular decisions
working for change

Chapter Summary

I. Factors That Foster Change

Change is inevitable and is an ongoing process that can be met with resistance or support. Change must be anticipated whenever possible. First-line supervisors deal with change on a daily basis. Dealing with change requires many skills, including communication, motivation, team building, and leadership.

Change is occurring in society, in the organization, and in individuals. Supervisors must recognize that there is a need to change leadership styles to fit the changes occurring in policing.

II. Police Unions

One result of changing values has been increased support of labor unions. Approximately 73 percent of the police officers in the United States are represented by a form of association or union. Police unions have been successful in allowing officers to: (1) have an input in the future, (2) provide for economic security, and (3) challenge the autocratic power of police managers.

A. *Collective Bargaining.* A process by which the department and the union negotiate a formal written agreement about wages, hours, and working conditions.

First-line supervisors function as part of the management team, which separates them from line officers in labor issues.

III. The Law

Some of the problems facing police officers today include ambiguity and vagueness of the law, laws that are obsolete and outmoded, and political pressure that alters the enforcement of certain crimes. Such problems create frustration and job dissatisfaction in officers, due to the spontaneous decision-making process that they are exposed to on the job. The officer must enforce the law and then accept the consequences if his or her decision is questioned.

IV. Positive Aspects of Change

First-line supervisors interpret policies and serve as spokespeople for management. The sergeant whose style is objective and fair and shows concern for officers will find less resistance to change. The first-line supervisor is responsible for identifying the key variables within their subordinates that create job satisfaction. These can include:

1.	Accomplishment	7.	Management
2.	Accountability	8.	Relationships
3.	Advancement	9.	Resources
4.	Challenge	10.	Supervision
5.	Comfort	11.	Workload
6.	Compensation		

These are important to identify, because they can help the supervisor in not only motivating the subordinate, but also in diffusing resistance to change.

Officers can be adaptable to change and will accept it more readily when included in the decision-making process. Reasons for accepting change include:

1. Choice
2. Improvement
3. Being informed
4. A need is satisfied
5. Planned change

V. Resistance to Change

Resistance to change can occur in many stages and for many reasons:

1. *Economic.* Wages and benefits that become threatened by either the chief administrators of the department or the politicians of the community will usually cause officers to unite, usually through associations or unions.

2. *Ambiguity is Created.* When the consequences of the change are either unknown or vague there is a greater potential for resistance.

3. *Relationships are Restricted.* If management attempts to restrict the social relationships or change organizational structure, it is usually met with resistance.

4. *Habits are Altered.* People become used to doing things a certain way and may resist if forced to change from familiar work patterns and habits.

5. *Discretion is Restricted or Eliminated.* Officers feel a sense of power when they utilize discretion and generally feel that excessive control over their discretion limits their effectiveness on the job.

6. *Unpopular Decisions.* When unpopular decisions are being carried out it is best to anticipate and prepare for resistance by providing justification for the decision.

7. *Cultural Reasons.* The paramilitary background of law enforcement supports conformity, therefore change is resisted merely because the organization itself fosters resistance to change.

VI. The Nature of Resistance

A. ***Rational resistance.*** Resistance to change may be valid. Rational resistance should be seen as a valuable part of the process of change because there might be a valid basis for resistance. By listening to the officers' resistance, the supervisor can alter the change, which will develop the trust and support of line officers if they know their opinion matters to management.

B. ***Emotional resistance.*** Resistance is usually for individual reasons, especially those identified with job satisfaction.

Deciding the basis for the resistance is important so that change can be approached correctly and proper alterations can take place. The supervisor will have an advantage in dealing with change if he or she is a part of the management team and involved in the planning that precedes change.

A. *Being Knowledgeable.* A supervisor needs to be armed with all the information available before presenting the issue of change. It is imperative that each alternative be considered and each advantage or disadvantage be examined. Change must be "sold" to officers so that resistance is reduced.

B. *Involvement.* If the people who will be most affected by the change are asked to participate in the implementation phase of the change, it provides the greatest chance of success. It sends a message to the other officers to accept the change.

C. *Communication.* Keeping channels of communication open will provide useful information for "selling" change. Open communication reduces resistance and reduces the problems that can arise from rumors.

D. *Informal leaders.* Informal leaders often can help implement change. They should be included in the process at the earliest stage of planning. They can influence the line officers because they are trusted.

E. *Mandated Change.* The first-line supervisor must be open and candid when mandated change is necessary. Supervisors should emphasize the positive aspects of change, reduce anxiety, and provide reliable information and a steadying influence. If the officers feel they can express their concerns to management, the resistance will be lessened.

Case Study Exercises/Essays

1. Assume you are Sergeant Hernandez:

    a.   Would you express your opinion about the proposed policy?
    b.   Would you talk about the problem with superiors?

2. Assume you are Sergeant Larson:

    a.   What agenda would you develop for your initial meeting with other supervisors?
    b.   Would you meet with individual officers before the initial meeting? Why?

Multiple-Choice Questions (Circle the best answer)

1. Change is:
    a.   static and cumulative.
    b.   avoidable with proper planning.
    c.   synergistic and cumulative.
    d.   negative.

2. It is the quality of _____ that takes priority in satisfying the need system of officers.
    a.   social life
    b.   work life
    c.   the labor agreement
    d.   the resources

3. According to Holton and Holton, the greater the _____, the greater the potential for resistance.
    a.   secrecy
    b.   ambiguity
    c.   change
    d.   unionization

4. The greater the _____, the more power is taken away from the line officer.
    a. ambiguity
    b. restricted social interaction
    c. power of the union
    d. control of discretion

5. _____ serve(s) to reduce resistance because the unknown becomes the known.
    a. Complete disclosure
    b. Involvement
    c. Written regulations
    d. Mandated change

6. Resistance to change can be lessened:
    a. as time passes and officers accept change.
    b. by mandating change.
    c. very little, as resistance to change is always expected.
    d. by integrating informal leaders.

7. _____ may be necessary when there is no time for, or success with, a consultative process of change.
    a. Mandated change
    b. Postponing change
    c. Absolute compliance
    d. Strict enforcement

True or False Questions

_T_   1. The larger and more bureaucratic a department is, the more it will resist change.

_T_   2. Team policing might be ineffective because power sharing may be viewed as a weakness.

_T_   3. Police unions are viewed by line officers as a way to challenge the autocratic power of police managers.

_T_   4. Officers are adaptable to change and will accept it readily when involved in the decision-making process.

_T_   5. Reasons for acceptance of change include improving work conditions and having a choice.

_F_   6. Resistance to change is usually individual and not collective.

_F_   7. There is no need for the supervisor to distinguish between rational and emotional resistance in order to effect a change.

_T_   8. To be effective in implementing change, a first-line supervisor must gather and assimilate the facts surrounding the change and identify the resistance leaders.

_T_   9. Efforts to restrict the flow of information can only enhance resistance to change and reinforce the informal organization.

_T_   10. Officers will normally resist change when it involves such things as restricted or eliminated discretion.

Chapter 10
Supervising the Difficult Employee—
Special Considerations

Learning Objectives

1. Describe a typical value statement for a police department.

2. List five characteristics of a problem employee.

3. Compare an ascendant employee with an ambivalent employee.

4. Identify the characteristics of an erudite employee.

5. Describe the type of employee who can be classified as a manipulator.

6. List the five types of problem employees.

7. Identify the view taken by most marginal employees.

8. Write a short essay describing work stressors.

9. List six task stressors.

10. Describe the nature and extent of suicide in law enforcement.

11. Identify the key elements of an early warning system.

12. Describe the types of problems that can be dealt with by an employee assistance program.

Key Concepts

alcohol
ambivalent employees
ascendant employees
critical-incident stress management
defeatists
departmental values
divorce
early warning systems
employee assistance program (EAP)
erudites
fitness-for-duty evaluations
indecisives

indifferent employees
manipulators
marginal performers
peer counseling
post-traumatic stress disorder
problem employees
suicide
task stressors
tyrants
value statements
work stressors

Chapter Summary

Today's supervisors must set the tone and lay a foundation for a strong and supportive work environment. Value statements set the tone for many organizations, representing ideals that serve as the foundation for policies, goals, and operations. They are reminders of the factors that contribute to a positive work environment.

I. Types of Employees

While it is not easy to categorize employees, organizations generally consist of three types of individuals. Employees must be viewed on an individual basis, but these generalized groups help in viewing employee conduct that is similar to other employees.

A. *Ascendant.* These employees are work-oriented, success-driven, and highly focused on their assignments. They are highly self-confident and like challenging assignments. They thrive on recognition and promotion. They are loners who generally think they are the only ones to accomplish tasks well. The negative side of this employee is that they are intolerant of other employees who do not work to their standards. Tasks will usually be done correctly and efficiently, with little need for supervision. Their allegiance is to the profession rather than the department.

B. *Indifferent.* These employees perform duties at an acceptable, minimal level. Their concentration is on getting by, and their focus is usually on family or nondepartmental activites. They do just enough to get by and avoid discipline, resisting any change. They are highly social with other officers and tend to strengthen informal work groups. They are difficult to supervise because motivational efforts have a short span, and they require close supervision.

C. *Ambivalent.* These officers are creative and intelligent. They will seek out critical areas of the job and gather knowledge about them. However, routine work becomes stagnant and boring, and they become procrastinators. As the frustration level increases, these officers become less decisive and resist any procedural changes. This employee may or may not seek upward mobility. However, if these employees receive challenging tasks, they are hardworking. They enjoy rewards and praise.

Supervisor expectations are critical to subordinate performance, and acceptable levels of job performance should be made clear to all employees. Setting high standards is necessary to receive high performance.

II. Problem Employees

Supervisors spend a great deal of time dealing with conflict and problem employees. Problem situations must be dealt with before they have a negative impact on other employees and the organiztion itself.

A. *Erudites.* These employees always have an opinion and see themselves as intellectuals. They show a low tolerance of other people, but they will follow departmental procedures. They will try to use their expertise to influence decisions. First-line supervisors need to guard against allowing them to take over as leaders.

B. *Tyrants.* These employees are control-oriented and fail to respect others. They will respond explosively and work at intimidating people. They want to control the situation and must win at all costs, even if they have to resort to coercion or fear. The supervisor must react to this employee by responding at the same level to maintain control and stop the employee's aggressive behavior. Any confrontation should be done privately and as often as necessary.

C. *Defeatists.* These employees are chronic complainers and resist every new idea. The first-line supervisor must force this employee to deal with specifics rather than generalizations. The first-line supervisor must confront this employee and make the employee explain his or her position, clarifying the situation and dealing with the specific problem.

D. *Manipulators.* These employees are unethical, thriving on half-truths and innuendo. They gather knowledge to build power. They focus on dividing and conquering and will pit one person against another in order to achieve their goal. If they can create enough conflict and confusion, they can manipulate others more effectively. The first-line supervisor must investigate each action taken by this person and then form an opinion based on facts to objectively refute the manipulator.

E. *Indecisives.* These employees do not like to make decisions and will avoid doing so at all costs. They rarely express their attitudes and beliefs and are expert procrastinators. They believe that if they do not give an opinion, they cannot be judged. The first-line supervisor should try to identify why these employees refuse to make decisions. This is best achieved by direct questioning to clarify areas of confusion and then requiring the officer to respond clearly about the problem. The supervisor should not settle for anything less than a direct answer.

III. The Marginal Performer

Marginal performers do just enough to get by. They perform tasks more slowly than normal and take advantage of things that benefit them directly, such as meal breaks and coffee breaks. They are usually late and will abuse sick time. They will work at giving themselves the appearance that they are working harder; however, it will be nonproductive work. Their complacency affects everything about their job, and their priorities are outside of their job. The are generally passive, not goal-oriented, and they do not accept responsibility for their lack of productivity. They simply blame management.

The first-line supervisor should set down goals for these employees, making sure to provide a plan to reach those goals. These employees need to understand their place within the organization and what makes up a working relationship. However, they need to receive praise and recognition for accomplishing tasks at an acceptable level. Timely positive reinforcement is important. The supervisor should have a positive attitude when dealing with these employees. However, if the employee fails to perform up to standards, the supervisor must document and take corrective action.

IV. Work Stressors

Employees are affected by both organizational and personal stress. Stress can have a negative or a positive effect. However, the supervisor should focus concern on the negative effects of the stress, which can affect an officer's ability to work. Stress can show its effects through low productivity, abuse of sick leave, and low morale. Over time, stress can lead to a variety of illnesses, mental and personal problems that can affect an officer's productivity, health, happiness—and can even be life-threatening.

A. *Task stressors.* Stress that can adversely affect the officer's work and personal life. The main stressors are:

1. danger
2. boredom
3. role conflict and ambiguity
4. control over work
5. shift work
6. use of excessive force

V. Personal Problems

Because of the close working relationship with officers, the first-line supervisor may receive information or officers may confide in the supervisor about personal stress. The supervisor may be able to help, or he or she may need to refer officers to an employee assistance program. Important problem areas include:

1.   suicide
2.   alcohol abuse
3.   divorce
4.   spousal concerns about danger

VI. Early Warning Systems

Many agencies have instituted early warning systems, which monitor officers' conduct and alert management to inappropriate behavior. The system is nondisciplinary in nature. Behavioral activities are monitored and officers at risk are identified for intervention. Responses might include counseling, training, referral to programs, psychological exams, physical exams, urinalysis, etc. Problems identified through this system are frequently resolved through employee assistance programs (EAPs).

VII. Employee Assistance Programs

An employee assistance program is a comprehensive program that may use in-house or external specialists. EAPs cover a wide range of services to help employees deal with emotional, family, psychological, financial, and retirement matters. Specialists work with the employee to get him or her back into the work environment and salvage the employee, if possible.

VIII. Critical-Incident Stress Management

A. *Post-Traumatic Stress Disorder*. A psychological condition caused by one's inability to successfully manage an emotional response triggered by severe trauma. PTSD has some typical symptoms that may serve as indicators. Early intervention after a critical incident can help to eliminate the chance of the response developing into post-traumatic stress disorder. It is very important that employees be debriefed after an incident.

B. *Peer Counseling.* A program that has proven to be successful because officers often do not want to admit they have a stress-related problem, and peer counselors are viewed as equals and thus are more likely to be trusted by fellow officers. Peer counselors should receive extensive training before attempting to deal with these serious problems. However, peer counselors have been highly successful in dealing with situations such as alcoholism, drug abuse, terminal illness, deaths, on-the-job injuries, and retirement.

IX. Fitness-for-Duty Evaluations

A fitness-for-duty evaluation may be appropriate when an officer's behavior calls into question his or her judgment, stability, self-control, or emotional control in performing duties as a police officer. There are also several guidelines set out by IACP for agencies to help deal with problems such as depression, anxiety, judgment problems and emotional control problems that the police agency may later be responsible for.

Case Study Exercises/Essays

1. Officer Hammonds has been on the force for 12 years and has recently divorced and lost custody of his children. Before his divorce he was just an average officer, but since then things have changed. He works all he can and works places moonlighting as well. His job performance has dramatically increased and his sergeant begins to wonder if he is sleeping at all. Assume you are Officer Hammonds' sergeant:

    a. Would you be concerned for Officer Hammonds?
    b. Would you document the changes you noticed and the reasons for those changes?

2. Corporal Stillwell is an officer of 10 years who has just been promoted. He received his promotion for being so specialized. He begins to act very arrogant around other officers, bragging about his intelligence. Assume you are Sergeant Jones:

    a. What actions would you take at this point?
    b. When would you intervene with Stillwell's ego and behavior?

Multiple-Choice Questions (Circle the best answer)

1. What are the three types of individuals in an organization?
    a. ascendant, indifferent, and marginal
    b. ascendant, indifferent, and ambivalent
    c. manipulators, tyrants, and indecisives
    d. ambitious, indecisive, and marginal

2. Suicide is more prevalent in the _____ population, and the same is true for the policing field.
    a. white female
    b. white male
    c. black female
    d. black male

3. According to *Law Enforcement News*, a study issued in 1994 concluded that the fundamental reasons officers committed suicide include all but which one of the following?
    a. despondency
    b. substance abuse
    c. personal problems
    d. job-related stress

4. For the marginal performer, which of the following is incorrect?
    a. never volunteer for any assignment
    b. primary interest is the department
    c. promotions are of little consequence
    d. top brass is viewed as being out-of-step with reality

5. The supervisor, when dealing with a marginal employee, should strive to deal with him or her on a:
    a. negative level.
    b. equal level.
    c. positive level.
    d. The supervisor should not deal with this employee, because the employee would view this as a weakness of the supervisor.

6. The organizational effects of work stressors include:
    a. violence.
    b. marital problems.
    c. accidents.
    d. irresponsibility.

7. The personal effects of work stressors include:
    a. increased errors.
    b. unpreparedness.
    c. irresponsibility.
    d. absenteeism.

8. _____ are the basis for beliefs and actions taken by a department.
    a. Foundations
    b. Policies
    c. Systems
    d. Values

9. _____ and _____ are two significant sources of stress for officers and the police organization, especially with the move toward community policing and an emphasis on solving community problems.
    a. Ambiguity, confusion
    b. Danger, workload
    c. Role conflict, ambiguity
    d. Budget, personnel

10. Evidence suggests that workload is not as critical to the health of a worker as the:
    a. control the worker has over work pace.
    b. elimination of shift work.
    c. alleviation of boredom.
    d. risk of injury.

11. Which of the following attitudes is *not* representative of the ambivalent employee?
    a. seeks approval and recognition
    b. does not like to make decisions
    c. reluctant to accept change
    d. creative and intelligent

12. The average day-shift worker gets _____ more hours of sleep weekly than the typical night-shift worker.
    a. 15
    b. 12
    c. eight
    d. four

13. Violanti, Marshall, and Howe (1985) suggest that _____ may be involved in the decision to use alcohol.
    a. psychosomatic diseases
    b. stress
    c. boredom
    d. job dissatisfaction

14. In 1996 there were more than 46,000 assaults on law enforcement officers, and in 1999 there were more than _____ assaults on officers.
    a. 65,000
    b. 76,000
    c. 55,000
    d. 85,000

15. According to Geller and Scott (1992), all but which of the following are factors used to assess an officer's propensity to misuse force?
    a. assignments, including partners and supervisors
    b. incidents resulting in injury
    c. absenteeism
    d. commendations and evaluations

16. Which of the following employee types is seldom at a loss for words, viewing himself as an intellectual in a class by himself?
    a. erudite
    b. manipulator
    c. expounder
    d. educated

17. Which of the following officer types is difficult to judge because she hides her attitudes and beliefs, remaining as neutral as possible?
    a. defeatist
    b. procrastinator
    c. ambivalent
    d. indecisive

18. Most officers in an organization are _____; they are imaginative and intelligent but easily bored by routine tasks, leading them to become procrastinators.
    a. ascendant
    b. ambivalent
    c. ambitious
    d. active

19. Problem employees are typically at which of the following points in their careers?
    a. Rookie officers having a difficult time adapting are the most problematic.
    b. After about five years on the job employees become frustrated with the sameness of their day-to-day routine, leading to problem behavior.
    c. Officers biding their time to retirement—who are past promotion opportunities and wanting to avoid dangerous situations—become problem employees.
    d. Inappropriate behavior can occur at any stage of an officer's employment, from newly appointed to retirement age.

True or False Questions

F   1. Supervisors are not required to change values and beliefs in efforts to set the tone, change the paradigms, and create foundations that result in a supportive work environment.

T   2. The first-line supervisor is the key if the changing organization is to become a learning organization.

T   3. Employees are responsible for results when they are part of the decision-making process.

T   4. Values are the basis for the beliefs and actions taken by a department.

F   5. According to More, Wegener, and Miller, "Each officer is a distinctive person with a team player personality."

F   6. An ascendant officer is imaginative, intelligent, and spends considerable time becoming knowledgeable about critical areas.

F   7. Ambivalent employees perform their duties at what they perceive as an acceptable level, which proves to be minimal.

F   8. Indifferent employees actively seek promotions.

T   9. When conflict is created by officers, the supervisor has to spend a considerable amount of time dealing with the conflict.

F   10. Performance problems require a supervisor to analyze the situation carefully, give advice, and if necessary order the officers to resolve the problem.

F   11. Problem behavior evolves from a personality conflict between a supervisor and an officer.

F   12. Specific task stressors in law enforcement are usually not wide-ranging, but they do include role conflict and ambiguity.

T   13. Employee assistance programs offer the same type of assistance that is given to those who have a physical illness.

F   14. The quality of a psychological work environment should be such that employees learn their role and have a desire to please their immediate supervisor.

Chapter 11
Internal Discipline—
A System of Accountability

Learning Objectives

1. Identify and describe several forms of police deviance.

2. Explore the basic concept of administrative responsibility.

3. Discuss the need for a formal internal investigation policy.

4. Examine the synergistic balance of factors required to keep police misconduct under control.

5. Differentiate between the sources of personnel complaints.

6. Identify three major types of police misconduct complaints.

7. List the steps involved in a police personnel investigation.

8. Examine the structure and function of a police trial board.

9. Develop an appreciation for the importance of procedural due process.

10. Understand how complaint dispositions should be classified.

11. Explore the various roles played by the sergeant in the administration of internal discipline.

12. Discuss the role of the chief police executive in providing leadership for and control of the disciplinary system.

13. Examine the relationship between the early warning system, the employee assistance program, and Total Quality Management of police personnel.

Key Concepts

adjudication
complaint receipt
disciplinary action
dispositions
due process
early warning system (EWS)
employee assistance program (EAP)
executive leadership
fairness
internal discipline
occupational deviance

participation
personnel complaints
police deviance
police misconduct
proactive policy
professionalism
responsibility
supervisor's role
trial boards

Chapter Summary

I. Police Work

Police work has become highly complex, with the majority of an officer's time spent keeping the peace and providing nonpolice services. Even though it can be rewarding, police work is often also unappreciated and unpleasant. Due to broad discretionary power, the complexity of their work, and some of the people that the work requires officers to come into contact with, police are particularly vulnerable to corruption and deviance.

    A. ***Police deviance.*** Activities that are inconsistent with an officer's legal authority, organizational authority, or standards of ethical conduct.

    B. ***Corruption.*** Refers to the sale of legitimate authority for personal gain.

Occupational deviance has been classified into three categories:

1. *Nonfeasance.* Failure to take appropriate action as required by law or department policy.

2. *Misfeasance.* Performing a required and lawful task in an unacceptable, inappropriate, or unprofessional manner.

3. *Malfeasance.* Wrongdoing or illegal conduct that is dependent on or related to the misuse of legitimate authority.

Occupational deviance includes:

1. Corruption
2. Unlawful use of force
3. Mistreatment of prisoners
4. Discrimination
5. Illegal search and seizure
6. Perjury
7. Planting of evidence
8. Other misconduct committed under the color of police authority

Researchers have identified five problem areas in urban policing that can be considered institutional preconditions for crime, corruption, and deviance:

1. Wide discretion
2. Low managerial visibility
3. Low public visibility
4. Peer group secrecy
5. Managerial secrecy

The most effective way to fight deviance and corruption is to build a strong supervisory structure. Sergeants must be empowered with the authority and the training to control the behavior of subordinates. First-line supervisors must make a proactive commitment to integrity.

Each officer must be consistently held accountable for poor on-the-job performance or inappropriate behavior. Management must set down realistic ethical and professional standards for supervisors to use to judge employees.

Police officers have a difficult time shedding the "superhero" image that comes from public perceptions. To maintain respect and the integrity of the department, management needs to have a strong system of continuous monitoring for accountability and internal discipline. This is not an easy task for management, as it requires:

1. Revising inadequate policies and procedures.
2. Correcting or separating from police service individuals who are found guilty of serious professional misconduct.

II. Controlling the Police

The concept of responsibility includes professional ethics, answerability, and accountability. The police are key to the safeguarding of the democratic process; thus, occupational deviance cannot be tolerated. These three ingredients are essential to police professionalism and have been incorporated into a new police code of conduct (see Figure 11.1). It is management's role and responsibility to develop and implement the policies and procedures, rules and regulations needed to take the ethics theory and turn it into practice. First-line supervisors must play an important part in making sure this internal discipline works properly. It is the chief executive officer who is responsible for the discipline and control of all subordinate personnel. Policing the police is imperative to gain or hold the respect of the community. This trust and respect from the community prevents civil unrest from erupting.

III. Personnel Complaint Investigation Policy

If the department implements a strong policy that clearly defines, prohibits, and encourages the reporting of occupational deviance, it is a giant step toward accountability. The control of discretion is essential.

Police managers should proactively seek out deviant behavior and investigate the substantive complaints made against officers. However, police officers must fully understand the regulations if they are to follow them. Policy must be written so that it is clear and not overly rigid, yet it must strike a synergistic balance between managerial control, community expectations, professional ethics, and discretionary flexibility (see Figure 11.2). Procedures for investigating personnel will vary depending on the origin, nature, and seriousness of the allegation. The text lists seven basic steps of a more structured and formal procedure needed for serious complaints.

IV. Personnel Complaints

A. *Personnel complaint.* A formal accusation alleging that a specific employee is guilty of legal, moral, or professional misconduct.

Trivial complaints should be filtered out immediately and disposed of through proper administrative action. Complaints that have substance should be moved into the internal investigation process.

1. *Internal complaint.* A complaint that originates from within the department. These types of complaints are initiated by first-line supervisors or command-level officers who have witnessed occupational deviance. These complaints may also come from fellow officers who know or strongly suspect misconduct.

2. *External Complaints.* Come from outside the department from lawyers, pressure groups, elected officials, relatives, and others who have chosen to focus on police misconduct.

A first-line supervisor must be concerned about due process. The supervisor must determine whether a complaint is legitimate and accurate. Complaints offer supervisors and management excellent feedback by increasing awareness of potential problem areas. Legitimate complaints should not be discouraged, because they support the department's commitment to police their own.

The processing of the complaint should include:

1.   Verification that the complaint was received, along with an explanation of the investigation and appeal processes.

2.   Informing the public of the complaint and investigation procedures.

3.   Notifying complainant of the final disposition.

4.   Logging in the complaint and forwarding a copy to the chief.

5.   Maintaining complete records of the case. Publishing statistical summaries for personnel and the public.

There are three types of complaints:

1.   *Primary Complaint.* Received directly from the victim.

2.   *Secondary Complaint.* Received from persons who are not the victims but who are complaining on behalf of others.

3.   *Anonymous.* Complaints of occupational deviance from an unidentified source. Anonymous complaints should be handled with the greatest care due to the possible impact on morale of those involved. However, management cannot afford to dismiss these complaints simply because the source is unidentified.

V. Personnel Complaint Investigations

Because of the wide range in size and sophistication of the more than 17,000 law enforcement agencies in the United States, it is difficult to state the sergeant's typical role in personnel complaint investigations. But because sergeants are often the most visible and approachable of the management team, it is likely that most complaints of misconduct will be channeled through them.

Depending on their authority, sergeants monitor performance and serve as departmental disciplinarians. In minor cases involving police deviance they may bring charges, investigate, adjudicate, and punish subordinates when appropriate—subject to administrative review and consistent with departmental policy, civil service regulations, collective bargaining agreements, and the law. Investigating alleged police misconduct requires a great deal of skill, and the person performing this task needs specific training, guidance, and support. Internal investigation procedures should be swift, certain, fair, and lawful.

Once a formal personnel complaint is placed into the internal investigation process, official fact-finding begins. The tools and techniques used to investigate police misconduct should not differ from those used in other types of investigations. The first step is to interview the complainant to gather information, identify witnesses and leads, assess the complainant's credibility, determine merits of the accusation, and ascertain any possible motives by the complainant. The investigator should be discreet and skillful in handling the complainant interview, being careful not to reveal information or prejudge the case. It is important to keep written records that are clear, concise, accurate, and factual.

First-line supervisors and other internal personnel complaint investigators should be familiar with administrative and constitutional rules governing procedural due process, which protect officers who are not guilty and make sure that those who are guilty are treated fairly. Once the complainant interview reveals a need to proceed with an investigation, this investigation should be expedited. Delays hamper inquiry, lower employee morale, and erode public confidence in the police force. After all relevant evidence has been gathered and evaluated, the investigating officer must try to determine a way to prove or disprove the allegation, and the findings should be included in a comprehensive investigation report that includes a recommendation for disposition of the case that is then forwarded to the appropriate person for action. Internal investigations should be concluded within 30 days.

Administrative procedure should not be a substitute for criminal prosecution when criminal misconduct is determined.

VI. The Adjudication of Personnel Complaints

The chief administrator is responsible for determining the final disposition of all complaints. Personnel complaint dispositions are classified into one of the following:

1. *Sustained* indicates, based on the facts obtained, that the accused committed all or part of the alleged police misconduct.

2. *Not sustained* means that the investigation produced insufficient evidence to prove or disprove the allegation and that the matter is being resolved in favor of the employee.

3. *Exonerated* denotes that the alleged act or omission occurred, but was in fact legal, proper, and necessary.

4. *Unfounded* is used when the alleged police misconduct did not occur and the complaint was false.

5. *Misconduct not based on original complaint* means that while there was misconduct by the police officer, it was separate and distinct from that alleged in the original complaint.

If the complaint was investigated by someone other than the first-line supervisor, the sergeant should be contacted before final disposition is made. The sergeant's input should be carefully evaluated for objectivity and consistency; however, this is the best person to evaluate an officer's overall job performance, professional conduct, and value as an employee.

It is recommended by Nathan Iannone that the safest way to protect the department from civil liability in cases involving serious legal, moral, or professional misconduct is to follow the Supreme Court decision in *Morrissey v. Brewer*, which identifies the minimum requirements of procedural due process to which officers are entitled.

Many police departments have developed some type of trial board system to help make decisions in internal discipline cases. These boards are administrative in nature and are meant to provide a "neutral and detached" body that is expected to use rational, objective, and analytical reasoning in reaching a decision. Their role is strictly advisory. This board must be carefully monitored and managed in order for it to remain effective.

VII. The Civilian Review Movement

This movement has resurrected itself again and is based on the need for accountability of the police department. This group usually has no power to discipline, but it brings openness, raises issues of concern, and marshals public sentiment. Many officers and unions oppose outside review of any sort, and it is yet to be seen if civilian review boards will survive.

VIII. Forecasting and Dealing with Potential Disciplinary Problems

Forecasting potential employees prone to misconduct has become a popular management tool. The ***early warning system*** is structured to track complaints in order to flag potential problem employees and leads to a key interview with the employee. When appropriate, managers may recommend help in the form of coaching, counseling, professional care, or referral to an ***employee assistance program***. The early warning system is diagnostic and help-oriented rather than punitive.

Based on the assumption that it is more humane and cost-effective to salvage an existing human resource, EAPs provide opportunities for intervention and remediation.

Case Study Exercises/Essays

1. You are Sergeant Wilcox, and you have been in patrol for the last five years. You have now been a sergeant for three months and are starting to wonder about some strange things you are noticing. You notice people are lying on their reports about what happened at a particular incident or even about drug searches without probable cause. You ask Sergeant Weems for advice:

   a. How would you respond to the advice given by Sergeant Weems?
   b. If you were the sergeant, what would you do or say to the officers who are lying on their reports?

2. Sergeant Patterson is a shift supervisor at a small police department. One of his officers has been said to be next in line for a criminal investigator position. Patterson is leery of letting the officer, Tim Payne, go to CI because he has noticed when he handles a robbery or larceny extra things come up missing that were not originally reported. There have been many complaints of missing items in cases that Payne has worked but there is no proof to back it up. Assume you are Sergeant Patterson:

   a. How would you deal with the situation?
   b. How might you go about obtaining evidence against Officer Payne?

Multiple-Choice Questions (Circle the best answer)

1. _____ , secrecy, and lack of supervision are three important factors leading to police deviance.
   a. Violence
   b. Ignorance
   c. Peer pressure
   d. Discretion

2. Responsibility encompasses professional ethics, answerability, and:
   a. society's expectations.
   b. regulations.
   c. commitment.
   d. accountability.

3. The _____ is ultimately responsible for the discipline and control of all subordinate personnel.
   a. chief executive officer
   b. district attorney
   c. first-line supervisor
   d. precinct captain

4. Sergeants have a/an _____ and _____ obligation to accept and investigate all legitimate allegations of personal or professional misconduct.
   a. ethical, functional
   b. managerial, functional
   c. ethical, managerial
   d. lawful, functional

5. Performing a required and lawful task in an unacceptable, inappropriate, or unprofessional manner describes:
    a. malfeasance.
    b. misfeasance.
    c. corruption.
    d. misconduct.

6. The internal affairs investigation process must be _____ , _____ , _____ , and lawful.
    a. positive, swift, certain
    b. swift, certain, fair
    c. positive, swift, formal
    d. swift, fair, anonymous

7. The investigative effort expended on any internal discipline complaint should be at least equal to the effort expended in the investigation of a _____ crime where a suspect is known.
    a. felony
    b. misdemeanor

8. The first step in a personnel investigation is to:
    a. commit the police department to a particular course of action regarding the internal investigation.
    b. indicate one's personal professional opinion on the matter.
    c. prejudge the validity of the complainant.
    d. interview the complainant.

9. Personnel complaints filed anonymously should be:
    a. discounted as invalid.
    b. judged on their own merit.
    c. ignored.

10. A police employee whose internal investigation complaint has been sustained should be allowed to appeal a chief executive's decision and the police agency should:
    a. provide the resources for the appeal.
    b. provide the funds for the appeal.
    c. not provide the resources or the funds for the appeal.

11. Which of the following dispositions is added to the five-category system, giving the chief executive officer more latitude and flexibility?
    a. sustained
    b. exonerated
    c. misconduct not based on original complaint
    d. not sustained
    e. unfounded

12. When an internal discipline complaint is sustained, which of the following is more frequently used in serious misconduct cases?
    a. reassignment
    b. loss of time
    c. psychological counseling
    d. participation in a multipurpose employee assistance program

13. Police officers who, because of alcohol or other drug abuse, cannot function temporarily should be:
    a.   suspended without pay immediately.
    b.   taken home by the supervisor and dealt with later.
    c.   arrested and booked.
    d.   taken to the chief executive officer by the supervisor.

14. According to Iannone (1984), almost any _____ order to an employee is enforceable administratively.
    a.   lawful
    b.   reasonable
    c.   direct
    d.   indirect

15. Nathan Iannone suggests that the safest way to avoid reversal and civil liability in internal discipline cases involving legal, moral, or professional misconduct is to adhere to the requirements outlined in:
    a.   *Morrissey v. Brewer.*
    b.   *Morrison v. Bakke.*
    c.   *Morrow v. Brown.*
    d.   *Morley v. Brooks.*

16. The Supreme Court case mentioned in question 15 outlines:
    a.   a new police code of conduct.
    b.   minimum requirements of procedural due process.
    c.   legal obligations of the management.
    d.   constitutional rights and obligations.

17. The renewed interest in civilian review boards is referred to as a/an _____ movement in the text.
    a.   futile
    b.   advocacy
    c.   innovative
    d.   accountability

18. According to More, Wegener, and Miller, ideally the administrative trial board should consist of _____ police officers from within the department.
    a.   seven
    b.   six
    c.   five
    d.   four

19. The trial board members are responsible for determining _____ and making a recommendation to the chief executive.
    a.   innocence
    b.   guilt
    c.   fact
    d.   law

20. Decisions of the trial board should be based on:
    a.   proof beyond a reasonable doubt.
    b.   a preponderance of the evidence.
    c.   clear and convincing evidence.
    d.   a modicum of evidence.

21. According to the text, which of the following cities' trial board became so bad that the city had to seek state legislative relief to correct the problem?
    a. Los Angeles
    b. Chicago
    c. New York
    d. Pittsburgh

22. In an effort to minimize the need for formal disciplinary action in cases involving noncriminal and less serious police deviance, departments are experimenting with:
    a. coaching and counseling.
    b. employee assistance programs and early warning systems.
    c. retraining.
    d. extended probation.

True or False Questions

_T_   1. Police represent the fine line that separates freedom from chaos and legitimate social control from tyranny.

_F_   2. According to Mark Baker (1985), police officers are a composite of their unique experiences and they are different from the people they police.

_F_   3. Corruption deals with illegal acts.

_F_   4. Police administrators and civilian review boards are responsible for policing the police.

_F_   5. Researchers have identified seven basic problems in urban policing that they regard as institutional preconditions for police crime, corruption, and occupational deviance.

_T_   6. Supervisors and managers must make an up-front and proactive commitment to integrity.

_T_   7. Ethical ambiguity permits the police to operate in a vacuum.

_T_   8. The principal function of police is the safeguarding of the democratic process.

_T_   9. First-line supervisors are the operating engineers who make sure the internal discipline apparatus works properly.

_F_   10. Policy creates unrealistic parameters that control the use of discretion in complex criminal justice organizations.

_T_   11. It is no longer sufficient to only react to complaints initiated by those outside the organization.

_F_   12. The internal discipline system should be based on essential fairness and be bound by formal procedures such as are used in criminal trials.

_T_   13. The control of discretion is absolutely essential if the department is to protect the accused employee from unfounded or malicious allegations of occupational deviance.

_F_   14. A police department's personnel complaint investigation policy should be written to cover every possible contingency to protect the accused employee and the department.

_F_   15. The written personnel complaint investigation policy statement must be carefully crafted to strike a simplistic balance between managerial control and officers' expectations.

_F_   16. Misconduct complaints lodged against police officers come from three sources.

_F_   17. According to Iannone, some of the most frivolous complaints of police misconduct have been brought to light by anonymous information.

Chapter 12
Labor Relations—
Problem Solving through Constructive Conflict

Learning Objectives

1. Explore the hidden revolution in police labor relations.

2. Define *collective bargaining* and outline the steps involved in choosing a bargaining agent.

3. Describe *constructive conflict* and understand its relationship to participatory management.

4. Recognize management rights.

5. Understand the need for a strong management rights clause.

6. Identify goals that unions seek to achieve through bargaining.

7. Compare and contrast the methods used to resolve impasses in contract negotiations.

8. Define *job action* and describe those that have been used in police work.

9. Define the word *contract* based on its meaning in labor law.

10. Contrast *collective bargaining* with *contract administration*.

11. Identify the sergeant's unique role in labor relations and contract administration.

12. Appreciate the need for and value of a dynamic balance between labor and management.

13. Recognize the subtle shift from the traditional to an interest-based collective bargaining process.

Key Concepts

balance through constructive conflict
bargaining in good faith
choosing a bargaining agent
compulsory binding arbitration
exclusive bargaining agent
grievance
impasse resolution techniques
management rights/union responsibility
negotiating a CBA or contract
noneconomic issues

participatory management by contracts
role conflict and its impact on morale
scope of bargaining
sergeants as contract administrators
sergeants as disciplinarians
traditional versus "innovative" bargaining
unionism—the hidden revolution
union security measures
wages, hours, and conditions of employment

Chapter Summary

Labor unions were banned in the United States until the mid-1930s with the passing of The Wagner Act, known as the National Labor Relations Act. However, government employees were specifically denied the right to collective bargaining, and they became increasingly militant in their demands for equal treatment in labor relations. The Boston police strike of 1919 was a landmark event that exposed the nation to governmental labor problems. The strike failed to meet its objectives, but it made officials sit up and take notice, toughening their stance against the collective bargaining process for public employees.

By the early 1940s an informal collective bargaining process had developed with limited success, but it was likewise crushed by legislation, court decisions, police officials, and politicians. Soon government employees formed union-like professional associations that lobbied for legislative changes. By 1959 some limited rights to bargain were granted to public employees in regard to wages, hours, and working conditions. Public Employee Relations Act 195, passed in the late 1960s, became the prototype for collective bargaining statutes throughout the United States by permitting strikes by public employees in nonsafety categories.

Today, approximately three-fourths of all American police officers are dues-paying members of labor unions. Many of these unions developed from social or fraternal organizations. No national labor organization represents the interests of all police personnel, but national labor organizations do have political power.

Unionism and collective bargaining by police officers have been referred to as the "hidden revolution." Collective bargaining has become a vehicle for problem solving through constructive conflict. Balanced power between the union and management is the key to successful collective bargaining.

I. Management Rights

Management rights refers to the decisions governing the conditions of employment over which management claims to have exclusive jurisdiction.

1. *Reserved Rights Concept.* Presumes that management authority is supreme in all matters except what is expressly conceded in the collective bargaining agreement or where authority is restricted by law. Thus, little or nothing is said about managment rights in the contract.

2. *Designated Rights Concept.* Intended to clarify and reinforce the rights claimed by management. A management rights clause is part of the bargaining agreement to reduce confusion and misunderstanding.

II. Understanding Labor Relations

Collective bargaining is hailed as being good for organizational growth and development. It is built on the premise that controlled conflict between management and labor is good and necessary.

A. *Collective bargaining.* The process by which a labor contract is negotiated and enforced between the employees' exclusive bargaining agent (union) and the state or local government operating the department. There is an affirmative duty to bargain, but neither side is obligated to accept a proposal or make a concession.

One of the first steps is for each side to select a negotiating team. The knowledge, skills, and dedication of the negotiators determines the quality of the agreement and sets the tone for future labor relations.

Because police officers are not covered by the National Labor Relations Act of 1935, state legislation usually authorizes collective bargaining, meaning that most states have a State Labor Relations Board (SLRB) to administer the law and regulate the process. Once the SLRB accepts a petition for selection of a bargaining unit, it determines the composition of the unit, usually looking for a commonality of interests. While unions should represent employees whose jobs are similar and who share common interests, unfortunately there has been little consistency in this regard. A formal hearing and election lead to the selection of the bargaining unit, and the SLRB must certify the results. *Certification of representation* attests to the fact that a majority of those in the bargaining unit voted for the union. *Certification of election results* attests to the fact that the employees in the bargaining unit voted against union representation.

A certified police union is the exclusive bargaining agent for all members of the bargaining unit, whether they belong to the union or not. Management cannot negotiate directly with anyone other than the exclusive bargaining agent. Most states prohibit unfair labor practices and strive to keep labor and management coequal in the collective bargaining process.

Once the bargaining teams are formed, they must reach a consensus on the scope of the bargaining—the issues to be discussed. Normally it is in management's interest to limit the scope of collective bargaining while organized labor wants everything placed on the table for discussion.

Three types of bargaining proposals are outlined by the authors:

1. *Mandatory subjects.* These subjects, such as disability pay, occupational safety, and minimum staffing requirements, clearly fall within the category of wages, hours, and other terms and conditions of employment.

2. *Voluntary subjects.* These subjects, such as health club memberships, volume discounts on group purchases, and new benefits for retirees, clearly fall outside the mandatory category but are brought to the table for voluntary consideration. The other party is not required to bargain on them or include them in the contract.

3. *Illegal subjects.* These subjects, such as union shop agreements, binding arbitration, and the right to strike, have been specifically prohibited by the public employee bargaining law.

Rights and responsibilities clauses are an integral component of the collective bargaining agreement. They are designed to limit the scope of bargaining and delineate the areas of mutual concern. The power that management retains is spelled out in ***a management rights clause***. A strong management rights clause gives management a great deal of control over the operation of the department. This along with a mutually acceptable no-strike impasse resolution process is an essential part of effective management strategy. Management rights clauses are usually negotiated along with an employee responsibility clause. Management rights and union responsibilities are the starting point for all future negotiations.

The basic purpose of bargaining is reaching a mutually acceptable agreement on the issues raised. Proposals are generally classified into four categories: (1) non-negotiable, (2) negotiable, (3) trade-off, or (4) expendable.

Once a particular issue is raised, the other team is obligated to respond in one of four ways: (1) accepted, (2) accepted with minor modification, (3) rejected, or (4) rejected with counterproposal. In order to bargain in good faith, an opponent cannot reject an issue, clause, or proposal without an explanation.

III. Union Goals

A union's goals usually fall into seven categories:

1. Wages and working conditions
2. Union security measures
3. Impasse resolution techniques
4. Meet-and-discuss provisions
5. Grievance procedures
6. Procedural due process
7. Job security and seniority

Two additional areas that have surfaced in recent years are:

1.   Officer safety regarding personnel deployment, workplace security, and equipment.
2.   Adequate insurance coverage and the maintenance of fully paid health care benefits for officers who have been injured on or retire from the job.

Union bargaining teams also place great importance on negotiating strong security measures in the form of dues checkoff, maintenance of membership, and compulsory participation. However, many states with "right-to-work" statutes outlaw most union security measures.

Impasse resolution techniques are used to prevent police strikes. The most common being used in law enforcement bargaining are:

1.   Mediation
2.   Fact-finding
3.   Final best offer arbitration
4.   Binding arbitration

Binding arbitration is the most popular method, its power to work found in the collective bargaining agreement, state law, local ordinances, jurisdictional policy, and court decisions.

Communication is the key to the collective bargaining process and successful conflict management. Meet-and-discuss sessions are the vehicle for participatory management.

IV. Dealing with Grievances

A. *Grievance.* A complaint arising out of the interpretation, application, or compliance with provisions of a collective bargaining agreement. Grievance procedures and due process are built into virtually every labor contract. Procedural due process is considered a must by all union members.

V. Impasse Resolution through Job Actions

Most police union goals are achieved at the bargaining table or through skillful political manipulation. When this fails, the union may resort to coercive strategy. While union leaders tend to oppose the tactical use of job actions, they know that job actions are often a necessary part of the process. A job action should always be the impasse resolution of last resort.

A. *Job action.* A calculated disruption in normally assigned duties. The purpose of job actions is to give the message that the collective bargaining process has broken down and that conflict is becoming unhealthy and disruptive. There are four basic types of job actions:

1.   No-confidence votes
2.   Work slowdowns
3.   Work speedups
4.   Work stoppages

While job actions may achieve the union's objectives, they create feelings of fear, anxiety, resentment, and betrayal in the community. The community will remember this fear long after the negotiation's issues or problems are over.

VI. Contract Administration

Signing a contract guarantees continuation of the collective bargaining relationship for the duration of the agreement. An important part of contract administration is dissemination of information to all members concerning anything affected by the new agreement. A police labor contract is a living document. The parties must work hard to interpret language, work out bugs, make adjustments, resolve problems through a formal grievance process, and reach ethical compromises that serve the interests of the employee, the department, and the community.

VII. Role of the Sergeant in Collective Bargaining

Sergeants are in a difficult position between management and labor. It is the sergeant who holds the key to the success of the contract. It is also the sergeant who must translate the labor policies into practice. The sergeant has the dual responsibility of helping subordinates and informing upper management of potential problems. The supervisor is the first to receive and resolve the grievances before they go to the command level. Inadequate supervisors feed the need for unions and cause labor relations to deteriorate.

First-line supervisors must understand labor relations and the positive aspect of *constructive conflict*. First-line supervisors facilitate communication, obtain cooperation, and coordinate day-to-day operations. Sergeants must realize that unresolved issues fester and help to destroy the purpose of policing. Considering the extensive job responsibilities that involve sergeants in planning, leading, controlling, and coaching subordinates, it is clear that they are a part of management.

VIII. Interest-Based Bargaining Process

A subtle shift appears to be underway, moving from traditional, position-based negotiations to innovative, win-win negotiations. Interest-based bargaining reduces confrontation and focuses on mutual interests rather than preconceived positions. This bargaining method is gaining popularity and could revolutionize the way management approaches labor relations. These negotiation sessions have two criteria:

1. Dynamic interaction among team members unencumbered by formal environmental arrangements or occupational status considerations.
2. Open and candid discussion of mutual interests or concerns with respect to a particular issue.

Case Study Exercises/Essays

1. Sergeant Bill Toomey has been on the force for more than 22 years. He has been a member of the collective bargaining unit since it was established nearly 15 years ago. The union is now upset that the number of sergeants on the unit are leaning more toward the other side of the table. They feel the sergeants do not have the best interests of the other officers in mind. Sergeant Toomey has been asked to talk to the state labor relations board on the matter. Assume you are Sergeant Toomey:

    a. What would you say to the board?
    b. Should there be a limit to the number of supervisors on the committee?

2. Assume you are Sergeant Emerson:

    a. What would be your first course of action?
    b. What do you think the arbitrator would decide?

Multiple-Choice Questions (Circle the best answer)

1. Which of the following acts, signed into law by President Franklin D. Roosevelt, was officially known as the National Labor Relations Act?
   a. Bosworth Act
   b. Baker Act
   c. Myers Act
   d. Wagner Act

2. In 1945 union membership for blue-collar industries reached an all-time high of ___ percent of the work-force.
   a. 16.1
   b. 22.8
   c. 35.5
   d. 40.3

3. According to *The World Almanac* (1993), it is now estimated that _____ percent of all American workers are represented by unions.
   a. 16.1
   b. 22.8
   c. 35.5
   d. 40.3

4. Public employees at all levels of government resented that they were systematically excluded from collective bargaining and considered it to be an unwarranted intrusion on their _____ Amendment right to freedom of association.
   a. First
   b. Third
   c. Fifth
   d. Tenth

5. The Boston police strike of _____ is viewed by many unionists as one of the most important events in police history, giving the nation its first real exposure to labor problems in municipal government.
   a. 1945
   b. 1933
   c. 1919
   d. 1965

6. In 1959, _____ became the first state to grant public employees a limited right to bargain with their employer for wages, hours, and working conditions.
   a. Alaska
   b. Alabama
   c. Massachusetts
   d. Wisconsin

7. At the present time, more than _____ percent of the states have adopted legislation that permits public employees to participate in collective bargaining.
   a. 60
   b. 70
   c. 80
   d. 90

8. According to Cole and Smith (2001), nearly _____ of all American police officers are dues-paying members of labor unions.
   a. one-fourth
   b. one-half
   c. three-fourths
   d. seven-eighths

9. Unionism and collective bargaining are referred to by Samuel Walker as:
   a. sowing the seeds of change.
   b. the hidden revolution.
   c. the wave of the future.
   d. the scope of bargaining.

10. Collective bargaining is a vehicle for problem solving through:
    a. the decision-making process.
    b. unilateral decision making.
    c. constructive conflict.
    d. vigorous debate.

11. Which of the three types of bargaining proposals deals with new benefits for retirees?
    a. mandatory subjects
    b. voluntary subjects
    c. illegal subjects

12. Which of the three types of bargaining proposals deals with binding arbitration?
    a. mandatory subjects
    b. voluntary subjects
    c. illegal subjects

13. Which of the three types of bargaining proposals deals with disability?
    a. mandatory subjects
    b. voluntary subjects
    c. illegal subjects

14. There are four basic categories of negotiating proposals. Which category includes items the negotiating team is willing to give up?
    a. tradeoff
    b. expendable
    c. nonnegotiable
    d. negotiable

15. There are four basic categories in negotiating proposals. Which category includes items the negotiating team would like to have, but on which it is willing to compromise?
    a. tradeoff
    b. expendable
    c. nonnegotiable
    d. negotiable

16. Which impasse resolution technique requires each side to submit a "final" offer, one of which will be binding?
    a. mediation
    b. fact-finding
    c. final best offer arbitration
    d. binding arbitration

17. Which impasse resolution technique involves the process of quasi-judicial hearings?
    a. mediation
    b. fact-finding
    c. final best offer arbitration
    d. binding arbitration

18. Which type of job action alters the normal pace of life and generates public demands for a return to the status quo?
    a. no-confidence votes
    b. work slowdowns
    c. work speedups
    d. work stoppages

19. Which type of job action is designed to create anxiety and disruption in the public, producing social stress and precipitating demands for acquiescence to the union?
    a. no-confidence votes
    b. work slowdowns
    c. work speedups
    d. work stoppages

20. Successful police work requires:
    a. communication, cooperation, and ideal conditions.
    b. communication, cooperation, and coordination.
    c. communication, cooperation, and consideration.
    d. communication, consideration, and ideal conditions.

21. Which approach to management rights issues presumes that management's authority is supreme in all matters except those specifically conceded?
    a. reserved rights concept
    b. designated rights concept

True or False Questions

_F_   1. The Myers Act was signed into law by Franklin D. Roosevelt in 1935.

_F_   2. The New York police strike of 1919 was the cause celebre that gave the nation its first real exposure to labor problems in municipal government.

_F_   3. The Pennsylvania Public Employee Act of 1947 required public employees to bargain collectively with their employers.

_T_   4. The Pennsylvania Public Employee Act of 1947 forbid any and all strikes by public employees.

T   5. The dramatic rise of membership in police unions can, in large measure, be attributed to an influx of younger police officers.

F   6. Police unions have been forced to focus on national concerns more than on local issues.

F   7. The Police Benevolent Association can legitimately claim to represent the interests of all police personnel in the United States.

F   8. Samuel Walker refers to unionism and collective bargaining as the "open revolution."

T   9. Collective bargaining is a vehicle for problem solving through constructive conflict.

T   10. One of the most important issues in labor relations relates to the scope of bargaining.

T   11. Balanced power is the key to success in collective bargaining.

T   12. An organization needs someone to take charge and give it a sense of direction.

F   13. The designated rights concept presumes that management's authority is supreme in all matters, except those that have been expressly conceded in the collective bargaining agreement, or where its authority is restricted by law.

F   14. The reserved rights concept is specifically intended to clarify and reinforce the rights claimed by management.

T   15. Collective bargaining is built on the assumption that a certain amount of controlled conflict is healthy.

T   16. Sergeants need to have a fairly comprehensive understanding of human behavior, work, workers, unions, and the collective bargaining process in order to do their job properly.

F   17. The National Labor Relations Act of 1935 covers police officers as public employees.

F   18. Certification of election results attests to the fact that the employees in the bargaining unit voted for the union.

T   19. The initial bargaining session is a prelude to participatory management in police work.

F   20. There is an affirmative duty to bargain; therefore, both sides are required to accept a proposal and make concessions.

T   21. Selectivity is a prerequisite for success.

F   22. A strong responsibility clause gives the police administration a great deal of control over the operation of the department.

F   23. A weak responsibility clause gives away too much power.

T   24. The basic purpose of bargaining is to reach a mutually acceptable agreement on the issues raised at the table.

_T_   25. The first session at the bargaining table almost always sets the tone for subsequent meetings.

_F_   26. Innovative negotiations are known as position-based negotiations.

_T_   27. In healthy police organizations, sergeants are assimilated into the management team.

_T_   28. Sergeants play a pivotal role in contract implementation and administration.

_F_   29. Adequate supervisory personnel react to crisis situations.

_F_   30. Interest-based negotiations will never represent the wave of the future.

Chapter 13
Supervising Minorities—
Respecting Individual and Cultural Differences

Learning Objectives

1. Explore white male dominance of police work in the United States.

2. Define de jure discrimination and contrast it with de facto discrimination.

3. Discuss and show the relationship among prejudice, stereotypes, and discrimination.

4. Examine Title VII and the Civil Rights Act of 1964 and the Equal Employment Opportunity Act (1972) in terms of their impact on equal employment opportunity in police work.

5. Identify the elements in affirmative action planning and explain the difference between a goal and a quota.

6. Describe the characteristics of a nondiscriminatory personnel selection process.

7. Understand how EEO/AA has changed the composition of the workforce and the implications for the future.

8. Discuss the importance of the sergeant's role in translating equal opportunity theory into practice.

9. List and discuss the traits that distinguish a promoted patrol officer from a competent supervisor when dealing with nontraditional police employees.

10. Discuss specific ways that a good first-line supervisor interacts with nontraditional employees in an effort to help develop their full potential.

11. Examine the components of the OUCH test and demonstrate its utility when it comes to supervising minorities.

12. Discuss the composition of protected classes based on the Civil Rights Act.

13. Explore the California approach to field training for first-line supervisors.

Key Concepts

affirmative action
bona fide occupational qualification
changing demographics
Civil Rights Act of 1964
competent and supportive supervisors
dealing with sexual harassment
discrimination
Equal Employment Opportunity Act
first-line supervisor's role
managing a more educated workforce

nondiscriminatory selection process
nondiscriminatory supervisors
the OUCH test applied to supervision
prejudice
protected classes
sexual diversity in the workforce
strategies for supervising minorities
supervising nontraditional employees
training supervisors to do their job
white male domination of police work

Chapter Summary

I. Coming to Grips with the Past

Until fairly recently, police departments were made up almost exclusively of politically conservative white males, primarily from the working class with a high school education and perhaps some military experience. Officers were hired to maintain the status quo. Police work and the composition of police departments have been undergoing gradual changes. However, police have often successfully used their political power to protect their turf when it came to minority hiring. It is crucial for departments to hire women and minorities in order to effectively police their communities. Participants in the criminal justice system must reflect the character of the community served.

Discrimination based on sex and race is a continuing problem in our society. Researcher Gary Johns believes that prejudgment based on previously acquired knowledge and past experience is normal. However, irrational categorization can stem from prejudgment in several forms:

1.   *Prejudice.* A negative attitude toward a group of people considered to be different or inferior based on observation and on ignorance, ethnocentrism, and xenophobia. Generalizations are applied to all members of a group despite individual differences.

2.   *Stereotype.* A set of group-shared and generally negative attitudes based on tradition, limited interaction, or ignorance that assigns similar undesirable attributes to all members of the "out" group.

3.   *Discrimination.* Discrimination refers to the negative and unfavorable treatment of people based on their membership in a minority group. It can involve acts or omissions that negatively affect the group in order to satisfy a prejudice.

Prejudice, stereotyping, and discrimination are usually by-products of uncontrolled ethnocentrism or xenophobia.

1.   *Ethnocentrism.* The natural tendency of human beings to view their own culture and customs as right and superior and to judge all others by those standards.

2.   *Xenophobia.* The irrational fear or hatred of strangers and other foreigners. Minorities are often considered strangers in their own land.

Minority group. A part of the population that differs from others in some characteristics and is often subjected to differential treatment.

The *Civil Rights Act of 1964* prohibited discrimination based on national origin, ethnic group, sex, creed, age, or race. *Title VII* of the act prohibits employers and unions from discriminating against employees in 15 areas. In 1966, the *Equal Employment Opportunity Commission (EEOC)* was created under authority of Title VII as a regulatory agency and authorized to set standards and establish guidelines for compliance with the Act. The *Equal Employment Opportunity Act of 1972* extended coverage of Title VII to all state and local governments with more than 15 employees and gave EEOC more authority to formulate policies, procedures, rules, and regulations designed to ensure compliance with the law.

Because these changes were not effecting a dramatic shift in the makeup of public service, and nontraditional employees were not making it into higher ranks, the EEOC adopted a positive *affirmative action* policy. These guidelines were designed to promote activism without creating "reverse discrimination." The process involved four steps:

1.   Analysis of major job categories to determine whether minorities were being underutilized.
2.   Development of goals, timetables, and affirmative actions to correct deficiences.
3.   Maintenance of a database to determine whether goals were being accomplished.
4.   Constant assessment to prevent the reintroduction of discriminatory practices.

However, the concept of quotas and preferential treatment based on race, color, national origin, and sex are contrary to the law. Because most police departments use testing in the hiring process, the Supreme Court ruled in *Griggs v. Duke Power Company* (1971) that screening tests must be:

1.   valid;
2.   reliable;
3.   job related; and
4.   based on bona fide occupational qualification.

This decision was meant to protect candidates from arbitrary and discriminatory screening. Some police departments have moved away from comprehensive written tests and use assessment centers, which use multiple assessment strategies that involve various techniques to screen candidates and have proven to be less discriminatory than any other preemployment screening procedures. However, this method requires a great deal of skill and is more costly.

II. The Changing Face of America

Clearly, women and minorities remain underrepresented at all levels despite aggressive equal opportunity and affirmative action programs.

Managers, including sergeants, must ensure that discrimination is not a factor in hiring and that nothing is in place to prohibit minority officers from getting or holding jobs. The employment of minorities should be a recruiting goal rather than a quota governing hiring, and the composition of the community should be the guide when recruiting.

Recruitment. A multi-dimensional process designed to encourage people to seek careers in police work and to seek individuals qualified to do the job.

III. Supervising Minorities

First-line supervisors are key to minority workers' success or failure. They must create an environment in which all employees can satisfy needs while they work together to meet the goals and objectives of the department. Effective supervisors will be sensitive to individual differences and cultural differences among employees. Supervisors should:

1.   be knowledgeable, approachable, and empathetic.
2.   learn to listen and understand an employee's point of view.
3.   communicate openly and honestly.
4.   expect minorities to "test" the department's philosophy on human relations and the supervisor's commitment to equal employment opportunity.
5.   practice introspection and be aware of personal attitudes.

Supervisors should put together a plan to motivate employees. This plan should include:

1. Make the work interesting.
2. Relate rewards to performance.
3. Provide valued rewards.
4. Treat employees as individuals.
5. Encourage participation and cooperation.
6. Explain why the action is being taken.
7. Provide accurate and timely feedback.

Minority police officers are not only subjected to the normal stressors of police work, but also to the additional stress of skepticism and rejection by fellow officers as well as not being fully accepted into the police culture. Female officers are subjected to additional and unique stressors:

1. Personal feelings of competence.
2. Perceptions of peers' view of competence.
3. Reluctant acceptance into the male-dominated police culture.
4. Unfavorable stereotypical reaction from citizens.
5. Sexual harassment.

Supervisors need to be extremely supportive of these officers. They should be firm, fair, and impartial. Sergeants are "change agents" who must work to rise above being merely promoted patrol officers. Managers must make a strong commitment to equal employment opportunities. The chief must set the stage and endorse a total no-nonsense policy to support equal employment opportunities, including continuous reinforcement.

IV. Dealing with Employees in a Protected Class

A. *Protected class*. A group of individuals who have been unfairly or illegally discriminated against in the past, or who are believed to be entitled to preferential consideration due to aspects of their life situation. This term is currently used as a classification based on employees' racial or ethnic origin, sex (gender or preference), age, physical status, and religion. A first-line supervisor should become very aware of employees that have minority status.

The OUCH test is probably the most informative for all actions of the supervisor:

1. **O**bjective
2. **U**niform in application
3. **C**onsistently applied
4. **H**ave job relatedness

The OUCH test is recognized as a standard used by management and courts to determine whether real discrimination has occurred.

V. Handling Sexual Harassment in the Workplace

Sexual harassment can take one of two forms:

A. *Quid Pro Quo Sexual Harassment*. An individual is forced to grant sexual favors in order to obtain, maintain, or improve employment status.

B. *Hostile Work Environment Sexual Harassment*. Employees are subjected to suggestive comments, photographs, jokes, obscene gestures, or unwanted physical contact. The conduct has four elements: (1) unwelcome, (2) sufficiently severe or pervasive to alter conditions of victim's employment and create an abusive environment, (3) perceived by the victim as hostile or abusive, or (4) creates an environment that a reasonable person would find hostile or abusive.

Management has not consistently been held liable for coworkers' sexual harassment. However, management must act in good faith, have a formal policy prohibiting sexual harassment, have a user-friendly and effective complaint procedure, and use appropriate disciplinary action in cases of sexual misconduct. The department can be held liable if a supervisor is in any way involved in harassment, and civil liability may arise if supervisors ignore harassment or fail to assist subordinates seeking a remedy. Supervisors need to help management spot, stop, and prevent sexual harassment.

VI. Supervising Gay and Lesbian Police Officers

Sergeants must realize that they need to help in facilitating a change in human relations by welcoming diversity. Supervisors must clearly be open and accepting, demonstrating empathy in order to understand and utilize the talents of homosexual employees. Supervisors are change agents and culture carriers; they must set the tone by acting as role models for personnel. They must adopt a viable personal strategy for facilitating change in the workplace culture.

VII. Managing a More Educated Workforce

More and more of today's sworn police personnel have more than two years of college eduation. College-educated officers tend to have greater strengths in many key areas than their non-college-educated counterparts; however, they also seem to experience more stress and are more likely to question orders, request more frequent reassignment, have lower morale and more absenteeism, and become more easily frustrated by bureaucratic procedures.

Supervisors need to empower their subordinates and thus expand their own influence as leaders. This comes through delegation and allowing meaningful participation in decision making. *Empowerment* leads to employees accepting responsibility for a job well done. Effective delegation leads to effective supervision, but effective delegation takes thought and preparation. The success or failure of empowerment depends on the commitment and human skills possessed by those seeking to implement it. Increased employee participation and effective delegation benefit the community, the police department, first-line supervisors, and employees.

Empowerment is essential in order to recruit and retain college-educated officers. Sergeants are the key to the empowerment process. They must believe that people are their greatest asset and reject the supervisor's traditional role as an overseer of "employees" in the workplace.

VIII. Training for the New Supervisor

Even if sergeants are committed to fairness and equal opportunity employment, they need training to develop the necessary skills. They should be given on-the-job coaching and evaluation by a certified trainer. Unfortunately, budgetary problems mean that training needs are often abandoned. However, supervisory training is necessary to lower the percentage of vicarious liability cases and to reduce potentially disruptive behavior involving nontraditional employees. Proactive police managers know that the only way to guard against these potential problems is to strengthen the rank of sergeant through selective promotion, upgraded supervisory training, and unequivocal support.

Case Study Exercises/Essays

1. Assume you are Sergeant Johnson:

    a. Would you have gone about the process of informing the other officers in the same manner?
    b. Would it have been more appropriate to have Officer Jackson at the meeting when he made the announcement?

2. Assume you are Sergeant Smalling:

    a. What would you do to judge if the test is fair for females?
    b. What would you do if the test is found to be discriminatory?

Multiple-Choice Questions (Circle the best answer)

1. William H. Parker referred to the security of the "womb" of the police society as the shell of:
    a. majorityism.
    b. minorityism.

2. The importance of attracting women and minority officers is:
    a. providing them with government jobs to meet quotas.
    b. effective policing.

3. Discrimination that is institutionalized by law is:
    a. de facto.
    b. de jure.

4. College-educated officers tend to experience _____ than their less educated colleagues.
    a. more stress
    b. greater enthusiasm
    c. higher morale
    d. less absenteeism

5. According to Gary Johns, _____ is normal human behavior.
    a. prejudice
    b. prejudgment
    c. bigotry
    d. stereotype

6. Negative and unfavorable treatment of people based on their membership in a particular group is:
    a. prejudice.
    b. stereotype.
    c. discrimination.
    d. xenophobia.

7. Group-shared negative attitudes based on tradition or ignorance that assign similar undesirable attributes to all members of the "out" group refers to:
    a. prejudgment.
    b. stereotype.
    c. discrimination.
    d. ethnocentrism.

8. A negative attitude toward a particular group considered different and inferior is:
    a. prejudice.
    b. stereotype.
    c. discrimination.
    d. bigotry.

9. Sexual harassment is prohibited by the:
    a. Civil Rights Act
    b. Quid Pro Quo Act
    c. Protected Class Act
    d. Equal Treatment Under the Law Act

10. The natural tendency of human beings to view their own culture and customs as right and superior and to judge all others by those standards is called:
    a. prejudice.
    b. discrimination.
    c. ethnocentrism.
    d. xenophobia.

11. The irrational fear or hatred of strangers and foreigners is called:
    a. ethnocentrism.
    b. discrimination.
    c. stereotype.
    d. xenophobia.

12. The Civil Rights Act of _____ prohibited discrimination based on national origin, ethnic group, creed, sex, race, or age.
    a. 1972
    b   1965
    c. 1964
    d. 1966

13. Title _____ of the Civil Rights Act prohibited employers and unions from discriminating against employees.
    a. IV
    b. VI
    c. VII
    d. VIII

14. Which of the following was created under the authority of Title VII as amended in 1966?
    a. Civil Rights Act
    b. Guidelines on Employee Selection Procedures
    c. Equal Employment Opportunity Commission
    d. Affirmative Action

15. Which of the following required employers to take positive steps to overcome present and past discrimination in order to achieve equal employment opportunity?
    a. Civil Rights Act
    b. Guidelines on Employee Selection Procedures
    c. Equal Employment Opportunity Commission
    d. Affirmative Action

16. Which guidelines adopted by the commission were designed to promote activism without creating the reverse discrimination prohibited by the Civil Rights Act?
    a.   Guidelines on Employee Selection Procedures
    b.   Equal Employment Opportunity Commission
    c.   Affirmative Action
    d.   Civil Rights Act

17. Which of the following stressed the need for "goals," "timetables," and "actions" designed to deal with discrimination?
    a.   Guidelines on Employee Selection Procedures
    b.   Equal Employment Selection Procedures
    c.   Affirmative Action
    d.   Civil Rights Act

18. Which of the following involved four basic steps that included continuous assessment of utilization patterns to prevent the reintroduction of discriminatory practices?
    a.   Guidelines on Employee Selection Procedures
    b.   Equal Employment Selection Procedures
    c.   Affirmative Action
    d.   Civil Rights Act

19. Which of the following court cases was used to force the Department of Public Safety of Alabama to hire one black trooper for each white trooper until 25 percent of all troopers were black?
    a.   *Brown v. Board of Education*
    b.   *Griggs v. Duke Power Company*
    c.   *NAACP v. Allen*
    d.   *NAACP v. Bakke*

20. The _____ decision protected police officers from arbitrary and discriminatory screening during testing procedures.
    a.   *Brown v. Board of Education*
    b.   *Griggs v. Duke Power Company*
    c.   *NAACP v. Allen*
    d.   *NAACP v. Bakke*

21. _____ occurs when individual employees are subjected to suggestive comments.
    a.   Quid pro quo sexual harassment
    b.   Hostile work environment sexual harassment

22. For hostile work environment sexual harassment, all of the following are elements except:
    a.   The conduct is unwelcome.
    b.   The conduct is perceived by the victim as hostile or abusive.
    c.   The victim is forced to grant sexual favors to maintain employment status.
    d.   The conduct is sufficiently severe or pervasive as to alter the conditions of the victim's employment and create an abusive work environment.

23. _____ substitutes self-supervision for traditional organizational control mechanisms.
    a.   Authority
    b.   Autonomy
    c.   Empowerment
    d.   Isolation

24. According to Carter, Sapp, and Stephens (1989), about _____ percent of all sworn officers have more than two years of college education.
    a. 40
    b. 50
    c. 60
    d. 80

True or False Questions

1. Sergeants must be objective and fair with those in protected classes, reactive in deterring the sexual harassment of female, gay, and lesbian officers.

2. Sergeants, as developers of police departments' human resources, act as overseers, not as coordinators.

3. No-win situations are the heart of the empowerment process.

4. New police sergeants will need extensive supervisory training and on-the-job coaching to be able to cope with the human relations challenges of the twenty-first century.

5. In a 1989 Police Executive Research Forum survey, police administrators reported that college-educated police officers have lower morale.

6. Apathy is the key to understanding and utilizing the talents of gay personnel.

7. If a supervisor actively participates in the harassment of an employee, the police department and the governmental entity of which it is a part can be held liable.

8. Empathic supervisors can quickly subvert an otherwise effective antiharassment policy.

9. Supportive and reactive supervisors are in a strategic position to assist other police managers in spotting and stopping sexual harassment.

10. Under Title VII of the Civil Rights Act, sexual harassment between coworkers produces employer liability and is considered an action of the employer.

11. *Brown v. Board of Education*, Kennedy's "Camelot," and the Johnson administration's desire to create a discrimination-free society fostered the desire to create what was called "a perfect society."

12. According to the federal government's policy on Affirmative Action, an employer is never required to hire a person who does not have the qualification needed to perform the job successfully.

13. Validity is the consistency with which any test yields accurate measurements.

14. Reliability simply means that the test measures what it is supposed to measure.

15. According to *The World Almanac* (1994), African-Americans may account for one-fourth of the nation's growth over the next 20 years.

_T_ 16. White male sergeants must understand that many of their nontraditional employees have been conditioned to expect the worst.

_F_ 17. Favoritism and privilege are absolutely essential in effective supervision.

_T_ 18. Effective supervision always begins with an awareness of the individual and cultural differences among employees.

_T_ 19. To do the job right, supervisors need technical, human, administrative, and problem-solving skills.

Chapter 14
Police Training—
An Investment in Human Resources

Learning Objectives

1. Define *training* and discuss its role in the development of human resources.

2. Describe and compare *preemployment*, *preservice* and *in-service* approaches to police training.

3. Examine the relationship between preparatory preemployment police training and the concept of profession.

4. Identify the philosophical planks that serve as a foundation for modern police training.

5. List the steps involved in the police training process.

6. Discuss *principles of learning* as they relate to the training of police personnel.

7. Identify the steps in the police training cycle.

8. Explore various methodologies that are used in police training.

9. Outline the sequence involved in an effective instructional protocol.

10. Develop an understanding of the reciprocal and synergistic relationship between supervision and training.

11. Explain why there is a need for supervisory training and how it might be integrated with on-the-job experience.

12. Define *civil liability* and explore how it can be mitigated by effective supervision and training.

13. Learn to appreciate the importance of documenting all police training activities.

Key Concepts

andragogy
civil liability
documentation of training
field training officer (FTO)
good faith
human resources
in-service training
instructional methods
instructional protocol
minimum standards
pedagogy
preemployment training
preservice training
principles of learning and teaching
professional status

programmed instruction
Project STAR
qualified immunity
respondeat superior
Section 1983
six philosophical planks
supervision as training
supervisory training
task analysis
Theory Y assumptions
training as supervision
training
training cycle
training movement
training process

Chapter Summary

History tells us that the motivating force behind the training movement was the perceived need to reform the police establishment. The scope of training was limited to only the essentials and was very slow to take off throughout the country. The Wickersham Commission in 1931 found that only 20 percent of 383 surveyed cities provided any kind of recruitment training. The commission called for the establishment of mandatory minimum police training standards. This call for training has been reiterated by a number of commissions and associations since that time. By 1988, all states had adopted some form of minimum training for newly hired police personnel. Trends indicate more emphasis on training in the future. The authors describe the police department as a synergistic collection of human beings who are organized and equipped to protect and serve the community. A department's most important resource is its personnel.

Time has shown that the efficiency, productivity, and effectiveness of a department depend on training. Training must be:

1.   relevant.
2.   job-related.
3.   focused on realities.

Training is an ongoing process. Law enforcement training should: (1) incorporate the appropriate mission statement and ethical considerations, and (2) focus on what the officer does on a daily basis. The department has the responsibility to develop all employees to their fullest.

Police work can be seen as an emerging profession, possessing to some degree each of the characteristics normally associated with a profession:

1.   Social grant of authority
2.   Autonomy of practice
3.   Systematic body of knowledge
4.   Ongoing education/training
5.   Self-regulation
6.   Code of ethics
7.   Service orientation

I. Formal Police Training Programs

Until recently, police training could be simply divided into two types:

1.   *Recruit training.* Designed for newly sworn police personnel who, having met all the minimum qualifications for appointment, were commissioned as police officers contingent on the successful completion of a basic preservice police training program.

2.   *In-service training.* Focusing almost exclusively on the occupational and professional development of certified police officers through various specialized job-related training programs.

A rather new concept in police training is **preparatory preemployment training,** an alternative approach to basic training based on a proprietary vocational education model in which a civilian trainee pays tuition and fees to cover the cost of training in an attempt to access a career in law enforcement. This is a radical shift in policy and very little has been written about it. At least 17 states already allow it in one form or another. As police work moves closer to professional status there should be an increasing emphasis on preparatory preemployment police training; however, these programs will need to be monitored carefully in order to assess their overall impact on the delivery of police services.

All states encourage, and most require, basic training for all municipal police personnel. Many larger and more progressive departments have adopted field training officer (FTO) programs, utilizing interested, experienced, and skilled officers for the post-academy training of all probationary police officers. Evaluations are based on actual job performance and not subjective judgment. The FTO concept is an alternative to traditional *pedagogy,* which is one-way transfer of information from instructor to student. The FTO concept is based in *andragogy,* which promotes the mutual involvement of students and instructors in a learning process stressing analytical and conceptual skills in practical problem-solving situations.

Because training must be viewed as an ongoing process, police officers must be given in-service training to help them maintain adequate performance and to develop and adapt to change. Effective in-service training is tailored to meet the needs of the trainee and to maximize learning.

II. The Training Process

Department-sponsored training strives to improve the officers' performance and to develop the officers' capacity to handle higher levels of responsibility. The six philosophical planks of training are:

1. Motivation plus acquired skills lead to positive action.
2. Learning is a complex process, dependent on the qualities presented by the individual, the training group, the teaching methods, the trainers, and the department.
3. Improvement is based on the complex factors involving individual learning, shared expectations, and the climate of the organization.
4. Training is the responsibility of the police department, the trainer, and the trainee.
5. Training is a continuous process for bettering human resources.
6. Training is a continuous process of team building.

Training is a consciously selected means to a particular end. Managers use training techniques to meet their objectives, which can be categorized as follows:

1. Orientation
2. Indoctrination
3. Dissemination
4. Skill acquisition
5. Problem solving

The success or failure of a training program depends on the following:

1. Relevance of the training
2. Instructional methodology used
3. Capacity and receptivity of the trainee
4. Teaching ability of the instructor

Training is expensive, and managers should identify real training needs and not just guess at them. *Project STAR* was one of the first task analyses involving police officers. It focused on the roles, tasks, and training needs of police personnel in several states. Project STAR led to other task analysis protocols for use in law enforcement.

In one project funded by the LEAA, researchers identified eight applicant traits as significant in order for applicants to become successful officers:

1. Directing others
2. Interpersonal skills
3. Perception

4.   Decision making
5.   Decisiveness
6.   Adaptability
7.   Oral communication
8.   Written communication

It is important to select performance objectives to give direction to the training process before selecting a training strategy that will produce the desired outcome. The elements of the training process include:

1.   Setting relevant, precise, achievable training objectives.
2.   Specifying the content of training curriculum via performance objectives.
3.   Selecting the most appropriate police training strategy.
4.   Adopting a suitable style and effective methodology for training.
5.   Measuring outcomes achieved by the participants in the program.
6.   Evaluating the training in terms of approach, content, and effectiveness.
7.   Factoring positive and negative feedback into the process.

Trainers should be aware of principles of learning and training, such as:

1.   Motivation
2.   Effect
3.   Individualism
4.   Relevancy
5.   Active learning
6.   Realism

7.   Primacy
8.   Recency
9.   Repetition
10.   Reinforcement
11.   Feedback

Supervisors and trainers could be more effective with training if they attempted to avoid the following errors:

1.   Trying to teach too much.
2.   Trying to teach too fast.
3.   Lack of communication about training plans.
4.   Failure to recognize individual differences.
5.   Failure to provide practice time.
6.   Failure to show employees the big picture.
7.   Failure to give positive reinforcement.
8.   Intimidation of employees.
9.   Lack of common vocabulary.
10.   The Pygmalion effect.

The four parts of the training cycle are:

1.   Identifying training needs.
2.   Preparing training objectives.
3.   Preparing the training program.
4.   Conducting and evaluating the training.

III. Training Methodologies

A. *Instructional methods* are the tools used by police trainers to accomplish their objectives in relation to the development of the department's personnel.

Instructional methods should be chosen to fit the people to be trained. They include:

1. On-the-job training
2. Lecture method
3. Self-directed study
4. Role playing
5. Programmed learning
6. Job rotation

Good trainers serve as developers of human resources. They respect individual differences, master the subject they teach, base their training on recognized rules of learning, and do their best to choose an appropriate training method. The instructional protocol is the key to the process: preparing, motivating, presenting, reviewing, applying, testing, and reinforcing learned behavior.

IV. The Police Sergeant's Role as a Trainer

As stated by the authors, the sergeant's role is to obtain results through people. Therefore, the sergeant becomes a primary instructor to his or her subordinates. This is accomplished through counseling, advising, coaching, and teaching. Effective first-line supervisors demonstrate what McGregor called a Theory Y orientation—making certain assumptions about human beings and allowing those assumptions to guide their behavior. This empathetic supervisory style treats police officers as professionals and emphasizes developing them to new levels.

Supervisors should monitor the professional growth and development of their subordinates. Being a good trainer requires ability, a positive attitude, human relations skills, training, and commitment to human resource development. Training has many benefits to the supervisor as well:

1. Getting to know your subordinates better.
2. Promoting good human relations.
3. Building the supervisor's self-esteem.
4. Furthering the supervisor's own career.
5. Gaining more time, because well-trained personnel need less correction.

V. Training First-Line Supervisors

Sergeants must be properly trained to handle the variety of tasks expected of them. Training is imperative to ensure that the sergeant is more than merely a promoted police officer. Proactive departments have a very positive attitude toward training and view training as an investment in the future. Citizens likewise need to recognize the value in investing in police training. Effective training will reduce the frequency and severity of mistakes, benefiting the community, the individual officer, and the department. Training is a catalyst for change and a step toward professional development.

VI. Civil Liability for Failure to Train Police Personnel

Courts have sent a clear message that managers must hire the right people, train them, and provide for proper supervision. This message makes training legally mandated. Officers and departments must understand that they can be sued, based on vicarious liability, for the wrongful acts of their subordinates. The major areas of concern are negligent employment, negligent supervision, and negligent training. The best defense is to provide effective training programs and adequate supervision. Failure to do so can lead to civil liability.

It is not enough to provide training; departments must prove that job-related training is sufficient and effective. Supervisors must be trained in documenting all informal and formal training. Adequate training records must include:

1.   individual training record forms;
2.   completed examinations and quizzes;
3.   hands-on performance demonstrations; and
4.   lesson plans.

Documentation, or the lack of it, can affect the results of a vicarious liability issue.

Case Study Exercises/Essays

1.   Assume you are Sergeant Lockhart:

    a.   What types of motivation techniques might you use to entice the officers to do the training and do it well?

    b.   How would you measure to see if the officers were learning anything from the training?

2.   Assume you are Sergeant Smith:

    a.   What would you do to handle the problem?

    b.   How would you answer Sergeant Stoots?

Multiple-Choice Questions (Circle the best answer)

1.   New York initiated formal police training in:
    a.   1908.
    b.   1897.
    c.   1930.
    d.   1977.

2.   In 1931 the _____ Commission found that only 20 percent of the 383 cities it surveyed provided any type of recruit training.
    a.   National Advisory
    b.   American Bar
    c.   Wickersham
    d.   President's

3. As of _____ , all states had adopted either voluntary or mandatory minimum training standards for newly hired police personnel.
   a.   1977
   b.   1990
   c.   1967
   d.   1988

4. The building blocks for a sound law enforcement training program are anchored by _____ common assumptions.
   a.   seven
   b.   six
   c.   three
   d.   two

5. Of the characteristics normally associated with a profession, _____ is where members exercise a great deal of discretion in their work and are not subject to criticism from outsiders.
   a.   a social grant of authority
   b.   autonomy of practice
   c.   self-regulation
   d.   a code of ethics

6. Of the characteristics normally associated with a profession, _____ is where members have the privilege to practice a special occupation.
   a.   a social grant of authority
   b.   autonomy of practice
   c.   self-regulation
   d.   a code of ethics

7. Of the characteristics normally associated with a profession, _____ is where members are expected to have special competence because they have acquired unique skills through education and training.
   a.   autonomy of practice
   b.   a systematic body of knowledge
   c.   ongoing education/training
   d.   a service orientation

8. Most police departments spend only about _____ percent of their budget for training.
   a.   seven
   b.   five
   c.   three
   d.   one

9. Which of the following adopted an administrative policy allowing preparatory preemployment police training in 1962?
   a.   President's Commission on Law Enforcement and Administration
   b.   National Advisory Commission on Criminal Justice Standards and Goals
   c.   Wickersham Commission
   d.   California Commission on Police Officer Standards and Training

10. Two areas of negligence that have been the prime source of litigation in recent years are negligent _____ and negligent training.
    a.   employment
    b.   supervision
    c.   behavior

11. In a national study of 144 police departments, it was found that _____ percent provided in-house training for first-line supervisors.
    a.   12
    b.   23
    c.   68
    d.   97

12. The text outlines four steps to a successful training effort. Which of the following is *not* one of these?
    a.   establishing recruitment exams
    b.   identifying training needs
    c.   preparing training objectives
    d.   preparing the training program

13. Researchers have isolated _____ traits or characteristics applicants need in order to become successful law enforcement officers.
    a.   15
    b.   10
    c.   nine
    d.   eight

14. Florida currently requires all sworn police personnel to obtain a minimum of _____ hours of in-service training every four years.
    a.   20
    b.   40
    c.   60
    d.   80

15. The FTO concept represents an alternative to traditional _____ , which involves the one-way transfer of knowledge from the instructor to the student.
    a.   pedagogy
    b.   andragogy

16. _____ promotes the mutual involvement of students and instructors in a learning process stressing analytical and conceptual skills in practical problem-solving situations.
    a.   Pedagogy
    b.   Andragogy

17. _____ is probably the most cost-effective means for developing the department's human resources.
    a.   The FTO
    b.   Role-playing
    c.   Programmed learning
    d.   Self-directed study

18. _____ is designed to help recruits and in-service personnel understand the work of the whole organization.
    a.   Empathetic training
    b.   On-the-job-training
    c.   Job rotation
    d.   Programmed learning

True or False Questions

F   1.   August Vollmer has long been recognized as one of the greatest reformers in modern police history.

T   2.   The motivating force behind the training movement was the perceived need to reform the police establishment.

T   3.   In reference to training, public interest was at times sacrificed for expediency.

F   4.   Police work is becoming less complex and rewarding.

F   5.   Selective recruitment, negative discipline, adequate supervision, and effective training shape the department's style of policing and help to ensure the quality of its service.

F   6.   Police training must be job-related and absolute.

T   7.   Well-trained police officers are competent and have confidence in themselves.

F   8.   Training is a costly investment in human resources and hinders police professionalism.

T   9.   Police officers cannot legitimately claim full professional status until they resolve the training dilemma.

F   10.   According to Whisenand and Rush, police officers have an obligation to help the department develop to its full potential.

F   11.   Training is a panacea and not a wise investment in the future.

T   12.   Training is a means to an end.

F   13.   Most supervisors learn their job from the formal training they receive.

F   14.   Documentation of training methods is useful but nonessential.

T   15.   Police supervisors can be sued for wrongful acts of their subordinates based on vicarious liability.

F   16.   The best defense against vicarious liability is a reactive strategy.

T   17.   Well-trained police officers feel good about themselves and see real value in their work.

_F_   18. Reactive police departments try to synthesize planning and training to assist supervisors in adopting a positive plan-ahead philosophy.

_T_   19. National commissions have failed to recommend the preparatory preemployment concept for police training.

_T_   20. Shepherd and Austin view preparatory preemployment police training as a pathway to professionalism.

_F_   21. Authoritarian sergeants have the most influence over their subordinates.

_T_   22. According to More, Wegener, and Miller, the sergeant's job is to obtain results through people.

_T_   23. The lecture method is the mainstay of classroom-based training.

_F_   24. Lecture is the most effective teaching method.

_T_   25. The success or failure of the training program will depend largely on the communication skills and teaching ability of the trainer.

Answer Key

Chapter 1
Multiple-Choice Questions
1. c
2. d
3. b
4. d
5. b
6. d
7. c
8. a
9. a
10. b
11. d
12. e
13. b
14. b
15. a
16. d
17. c
18. b
19. b
20. d
21. c

True or False
1. F
2. T
3. T
4. T
5. T
6. F
7. F
8. T
9. F
10. T
11. T
12. T
13. T
14. T
15. F

Chapter 2
Multiple-Choice Questions
1. b
2. c
3. c
4. a
5. d
6. c
7. a
8. c
9. b
10. b
11. b
12. c

True or False
1. F
2. T
3. T
4. T
5. F
6. F
7. F
8. T
9. T
10. F
11. T
12. T
13. F
14. F
15. T
16. F
17. T

Chapter 3
Multiple-Choice Questions
1. b
2. b
3. a
4. b
5. a
6. a
7. b
8. b
9. a
10. b
11. b
12. c
13. a
14. a
15. d
16. a
17. a
18. d
19. b
20. c
21. a
22. b
23. a
24. b
25. d
26. c
27. c

True or False
1. F
2. F
3. T
4. T
5. T
6. T
7. T
8. T
9. T
10. T
11. T
12. F
13. F
14. T
15. F
16. F

Chapter 4
Multiple-Choice Questions
1. d
2. d
3. b
4. a
5. c
6. c
7. b
8. d
9. c
10. a
11. b
12. d
13. b
14. a
15. a
16. d
17. a

True or False
1. T
2. T
3. T
4. T
5. T
6. T
7. T
8. T
9. F
10. T
11. T
12. F
13. T
14. F
15. F
16. T
17. T
18. T

Chapter 5
Multiple-Choice Questions
1. c
2. c
3. a
4. b
5. c
6. a
7. d
8. c
9. c
10. c
11. b
12. d
13. c
14. a
15. d

True or False
1. F
2. T
3. T
4. F
5. T
6. T
7. T
8. T
9. F
10. T
11. T
12. T
13. T
14. F
15. T
16. T
17. F
18. T
19. T

Chapter 6
Multiple-Choice Questions
1. a
2. b
3. c
4. d
5. c
6. d
7. c
8. b
9. c
10. d
11. b
12. d
13. b

True or False
1. T
2. T
3. T
4. T
5. T
6. T
7. F
8. T
9. T
10. F
11. T
12. T
13. T
14. T
15. T
16. T
17. F

Chapter 7
Multiple-Choice Questions

1. a
2. c
3. d
4. a
5. c
6. e
7. c
8. a
9. a
10. b
11. c
12. c
13. d
14. a
15. c
16. c
17. d
18. a
19. b

True or False

1. T
2. T
3. T
4. T
5. T
6. F
7. F
8. F
9. T
10. F
11. F
12. T

Chapter 8
Multiple-Choice Questions

1. b
2. a
3. a
4. b
5. b
6. a
7. c
8. d
9. d
10. d
11. a
12. b
13. b
14. c
15. a
16. c

True or False

1. F
2. F
3. F
4. T
5. T
6. T
7. T
8. T
9. T
10. F

Chapter 9
Multiple-Choice Questions

1. c
2. b
3. b
4. d
5. b
6. d
7. a

True or False

1. T
2. T
3. T
4. T
5. T
6. F
7. F
8. T
9. T
10. T

Chapter 10
Multiple-Choice Questions
1. b
2. b
3. d
4. b
5. c
6. c
7. c
8. d
9. c
10. a
11. c
12. c
13. b
14. c
15. c
16. a
17. d
18. b
19. d

True or False

1. F
2. T
3. T
4. T
5. F
6. F
7. F
8. F
9. T
10. F
11. F
12. F
13. T
14. F

Chapter 11
Multiple-Choice Questions
1. d
2. d
3. a
4. a
5. b
6. b
7. a
8. d
9. b
10. c
11. c
12. b
13. b
14. b
15. a
16. b
17. d
18. c
19. c
20. b
21. d
22. b

True or False
1. T
2. F
3. F
4. F
5. F
6. T
7. T
8. T
9. T
10. F
11. T
12. F
13. T
14. F
15. F
16. F
17. F

Chapter 12
Multiple-Choice Questions
1. d
2. c
3. a
4. a
5. c
6. d
7. c
8. c
9. b
10. c
11. b
12. c
13. a
14. b
15. d
16. c
17. b
18. c
19. c
20. b
21. a

True or False
1. F
2. F
3. F
4. T
5. T
6. F
7. F
8. F
9. T
10. T
11. T
12. T
13. F
14. F
15. T
16. T
17 F
18. F
19. T
20. F
21. T
22. F
23. F
24. T
25. T
26. F
27. T
28. T
29. F
30. F

Chapter 13
Multiple-Choice Questions
1. b
2. b
3. b
4. a
5. b
6. c
7. b
8. a
9. a
10. c
11. d
12. c
13. c
14. c
15. d
16. c
17. c
18. c
19. c
20. b
21. b
22. c
23. c
24. c

True or False
1. F
2. F
3. F
4. T
5. T
6. F
7. T
8. F
9. F
10. F
11. F
12. T
13. F
14. F
15. F
16. T
17. F
18. T
19. T

Chapter 14
Multiple-Choice Questions
1. b
2. c
3. d
4. d
5. b
6. a
7. b
8. d
9. d
10. b
11. d
12. a
13. d
14. b
15. a
16. b
17. d
18. c

True or False
1. F
2. T
3. T
4. F
5. F
6. F
7. T
8. F
9. T
10. F
11. F
12. T
13. F
14. F
15. T
16. F
17. T
18. F
19. T
20. T
21. F
22. T
23. T
24. F
25. T